WEVERY S
WOMAN'S
JESSENTIAL G
JOB HUNTING
& RESUME BOOK

EVERY WOMAN'S ESSENTIAL JOB HUNTING & RESUME BOOK

LAURA MORIN

BOB ADAMS, INC.
Holbrook, Massachusetts

Published by Bob Adams, Inc.
260 Center Street, Holbrook, MA 02343

ISBN: 1-55850-382-X

Printed in the United States of America.

J I H G F E D C B A

Library of Congress Cataloging-in-Publication Data
Morin, Laura
    Every woman's essential job hunting & resume book / Laura Morin.
        p.   cm.
    Includes bibliographical references and index.
    ISBN 1-55850-382-X
    1. Job hunting. 2. Résumés (Employment). 3. Vocational guidance. I. Title.
    HF5382.7.M684   1994
    650.14'082—dc20   94-15946
                                                                      CIP

This publication is designed to provide accurate and authoritative information with regard to the subject matter covered. It is sold with the understanding that the publisher is not engaged in rendering legal, accounting, or other professional advice. If legal advice or other expert assistance is required, the services of a competent professional person should be sought.
    — From a *Declaration of Principles* jointly adopted by a Committee of the American Bar Association and a Committee of Publishers and Associations

Cover design: Pete Gouck

This book is available at quantity discounts for bulk purchases.
For information, call 1-800-872-5627.

Dedication

To your future.

Acknowledgments

This book would not have been possible without the encouragement and help of many people, including Brandon Toropov, who was always generous with his expert editorial advice; Susan Beale, who contributed her usual top-notch production work; Wayne Jackson and Nancy Collins, for their hard work and enthusiasm for this project.

Special thanks to my parents, Deborah and Robert Morin, for always encouraging me to reach for the stars.

Contents

Part III: The Job Hunt

Part IV: The Interview

Part V: Career Planning

Introduction

Why a Job-hunting Book for Women?

Our mothers remember it well.

As recently as two decades ago, a woman who worked was clearly an exception to the rule—an aberration. Those who went against the grain had to choose a profession from a very short list and without much hope for advancement: secretary, waitress, teacher, nurse, airline attendant, store clerk. Today, the possibilities seem endless. As corporate America is calling out for new ideas and more participative management skills, large numbers of women are entering the work force in every conceivable position, from advertising exec to zoologist. More and more women are breaking into traditionally male-dominated occupations and, for the first time, advancing into the executive suite.

But in the midst of these exciting possibilities, many women are finding that the career game is still stacked against them. The reality is that women today earn only about 70 cents for every dollar a man makes for the same work—and experts predict that if all goes well, we *might* reach parity in 25 years. Buzzwords like 'discrimination,' 'sexual harassment,' 'glass ceilings,' and 'glass walls' ring all too familiar to many of us.

For all of our progress, women also face many challenges in the job market that men do not. Women typically lack the networking channels and other resources that men enjoy, and are often scrutinized more critically than other job seekers. At-home mothers and home-makers face the added difficulty of having to explain gaps in their employment history.

Despite all of this gloom and doom, it *is* still possible to find a terrific career that can last a lifetime. And as you can see, women need every extra edge we can get. This book is designed to help you do just that, by providing valuable job-search advice specifically tailored to your needs, including:

- Chapters for professional women moving up the career ladder, women changing careers, at-home moms reentering the job market, students and recent graduates, and homemakers entering the job market for the first time
- Over 85 resumes and cover letters used by real women to get real jobs
- The latest strategies for women in today's tough job market
- The 20 hottest careers for women today
- Proven advice, tips, and secrets from leading job-search experts

Throughout this book, I'll detail all of the essential aspects of a successful job search campaign. I encourage you to go through the following pages thoroughly and use it as a reference tool throughout your job search campaign.

So keep reading, and remember—you're on your way to a fabulous career!

Part I

Assessment

1

New Rules for Tough Times: Job Hunting in the New Era

As a rule, the best jobs do not go to the most qualified individuals; they generally go to the best job hunters. Even though you may compete with people who have stronger credentials, you can still get the job you want if you're willing to put in the extra effort necessary to out-shine the competition.

NEW TRENDS IN THE JOB MARKET

Once upon a time, "work" was a necessary evil people had to contend with, to get out of the way in order to go about the larger business of life. It was not meant to be interesting or ful-filling, nor was it even thought of in those terms. A worker, typically white male, learned a trade or studied a profession, found a company that he dedicated his career to, and worked hard until retirement. Surprisingly enough, all of this held true as recently as 20 years ago.

Not so anymore. The current work force is in tremendous upheaval. Solid middle-class jobs, the kind that allow a single worker to be the family breadwinner, have been disappear-ing in record numbers or are being replaced by low-wage positions. Traditionally well-pay-ing, blue-collar jobs are going abroad or suffering substantial pay drops, forcing millions to learn less lucrative new trades. Meanwhile, there are more workers than ever, with a record number of baby boomers and women joining the labor force in the 1980s. Consider these chilling statistics, provided by the U.S. Labor Department:

- Total employment growth is expected to slow between 1990 and 2005 to merely half its rate between 1975 and 1990.
- Major corporations eliminated 50,000 jobs a month in 1993.
- More than 40% of all employees work for companies that have recently downsized.

As if that's not bad enough, these trends are expected to continue and possibly worsen well into the next millennium.

WHAT YOU CAN EXPECT

What does all of this mean to you, as a job hunter? Does it mean that there aren't any good jobs left out there? Absolutely not. Although the job market may be sluggish relative to recent years, it is still growing. In other words, there may not be as many jobs to choose from, but there are still jobs available. Most job openings will result from replacement needs, as people leave their jobs to move up the career ladder, change careers, or retire. Thus, even occupations with little or no employment growth may still offer many job openings.

However, jobs will be tougher to find and you will be competing with more job seekers than ever. You may find that you have to apply to more than 100 companies just to get a single interview. You might have to apply to 200 to get a single job offer. What once took a matter of weeks may now take months. Effective job hunting simply takes more planning, energy, and effort these days. But if you have the know-how and you're willing to put in the time it takes to carefully map out your job hunt, you're already two steps ahead of the competition.

Don't let statistics scare you. Remember, you're only looking for one job; you have a considerable amount of control over what kind of job you get and how long it takes because you control how much effort you put into your job search campaign.

So roll up your sleeves and let's get to work!

2
Taking Inventory

Beginning a new job search can seem almost overwhelming at times. One way to combat that feeling (and a very effective way to find a job) is to focus your search on a particular job or industry that you are especially qualified for, and that especially interests you. If you are happy with your current career or already have a strong sense of what type of job you want to pursue, go on to chapter 3. But if you feel as if you're still searching for "just the right job," read on.

FINDING YOUR FOCUS

One good way to find your focus is by deciding on the industry, job function, and geographic location of greatest value to you. Identifying these key elements will not only make your job search more manageable, it will greatly increase your chances of finding a job. Employers like job candidates who have real interests and a clear direction. They know that if you are interested in a particular industry, company, or job, you are more likely to enjoy that position, excel in it, and stay with the company for a good period of time. Employers do not like to hear that you aren't at all discriminating—that you'll take whatever job they have available.

PINPOINTING YOUR SKILLS AND INTERESTS

Think about your skills, talents, abilities, and experience. What are the best jobs you've had and the classes you've enjoyed most? What did you like about them? Consider your hobbies and interests. Why do they interest you? What are the activities or skills you'd like to develop further? What things do you do particularly well?

Now write down the details. Do not rush through this step—plan to spend a few hours taking inventory of your attributes. Be sure to include:

- Work experience (paid and unpaid)
- Volunteer experience
- Internships
- Education

- Other training (seminars, courses, licensing)
- Special skills and talents
- Awards and honors (academic, professional, and otherwise)
- Professional memberships and activities (such as professional associations)
- Social memberships and activities (such as treasurer of a local charity or member of the PTA)
- Notable accomplishments

Look over your list honestly and objectively. What are your strengths? Your weaknesses? What are your most marketable skills and talents? Your most notable accomplishments?

Think of your skills, abilities, and experience as a "product" you have to sell. What, exactly, is your product and what is most marketable about it? Once you determine this, ask yourself what industries or types of companies might want to "buy" your product. For instance, if after completing the above exercise you determine that you have excellent math skills, are very meticulous, and serve as the treasurer for a local charity, you might want to consider a job in accounting. Even if you have no prior work experience in this field, you already have some excellent credentials!

CONSIDERING THE DAILY TASKS

Once you've come up with a number of career possibilities, consider the daily tasks of each job and the daily tasks of the positions that it might lead to. Ask yourself if you really find the duties of that job interesting and if you would like to perform them on a daily basis.

Keep in mind that, on a daily basis, you will spend about as much time at your job as you do sleeping—so it's important to know that you'll enjoy the work before you decide on a particular type of employment. For instance, if you are thinking about becoming an elementary school teacher, you must first be sure that you enjoy spending a great deal of time with small children (who might test your patience!). If you are considering working in a retail store, you should like to work with the public, and be prepared to be on your feet all day and deal with dissatisfied customers. If you want to work for a daily newspaper, you must be sure that you can work well in a fast-paced, high-pressure, deadline-oriented environment. In other words, you need to be able to recognize the daily realities of your potential vocation and be able to see yourself fitting in to that work environment.

Try not to eliminate any occupation or industry before you learn more about it. Some jobs and industries evoke positive or negative images that aren't necessarily accurate. For some people, fashion designers seem glamorous while production occupations in manufacturing seem less attractive. Yet many a seamstress, pattern maker, or fabric assembler would be happy to report that their jobs are creative, flexible, and fulfilling. Jobs are often not what they first appear to be, and misconceptions are common.

Exciting jobs may have dull aspects, while less glamorous occupations may interest you once you learn more about them. For example, the opportunity to travel makes a flight attendant's job seem exciting, but the work is strenuous and tiring; flight attendants stand for long periods and must be friendly when they are tired and passengers are unpleasant. On the other hand, many people consider automotive assembly work dirty and dull; however, production workers in the motor vehicle manufacturing industry are among the highest paid laborers in the nation.

OTHER IMPORTANT CONSIDERATIONS

Bear in mind, too, that you are not just choosing a job, but a lifestyle. If you decide, for example, that your goal is to be a management consultant for an international firm, chances are you will be spending a great deal of your time in an airplane—so you'd better like to fly! Similarly, you should think about geographic location. Do you want a career that would require you to live in a large city, such as an urban engineer? Or would you rather live in a less populated, rural area? Consider such issues closely before you commit yourself to any one profession.

Think about the jobs you've enjoyed most, the classes you liked in school, and your hobbies and interests. Identify the activities or skills you'd like to develop further. Do you prefer to work alone or with a team? You may enjoy a work environment where there is a lot of teamwork and socializing, or where autonomy is the norm. What kinds of people do you like to work with? You may shine among imaginative people who like to brainstorm solutions, or you may do better with highly organized friends and co-workers who like to make data-driven decisions quickly.

Think about earnings potential—not only for the job you're considering, but for the positions it might lead to. Which do you feel is more important: to make a lot of money or to be fulfilled by your work? Think about your work schedule. If you want a job that allows you to have a flexible schedule, this will have a big impact on the type of job you can choose. If you are very ambitious and achievement-oriented, that's likely to mean that you will spend some time burning the midnight oil. How fast do you want to advance to your next job? In some careers and in some companies, there's a much greater chance that you will be able to advance quickly to a higher position than in other careers, companies, and positions. In some fields, the opportunities for advancement are virtually nonexistent.

You must also ask yourself whether the industry you are interested in is flourishing or dying. This isn't to say that you should jump into a particular field just because it's doing well, but the growth in a given field will probably have a major impact on your career prospects some years down the road. If the industry is flourishing, it could mean many more exciting challenges and better opportunities will be available to you—but it could also mean that you have chosen a much less stable profession, and will have to jump from one company to the next throughout your career. Sometimes it's a good idea to consider careers in industries that are slowing down or maturing—because they are more likely to have greater opportunities for advancement than industries that are booming and flooded with very talented young applicants.

Take into consideration whether the job function itself is flourishing or dying. Will the demand be increasing for the job, or is it slowing down? Again, you've got to consider not only what the competition will be like to get the job, but also what the competition will be like to advance.

Above all, keep in mind that first jobs do not necessarily reflect a person's career. A career is a long-term process that can take years to develop; the average person will have seven careers over the course of a lifetime. Rather than asking yourself, What is the job that's right for me? ask yourself, What would I like to try first?

GATHERING MORE INFORMATION

Once you identify an interest in an occupation or industry, you should gather more information about it, which will help you clarify if this is the right direction for you to pursue. This research will also help you later on in all stages of your job search, especially in the interviewing stage, where you will have a great advantage by being able to discuss your knowledge of the industry.

Your local library is a great place to find this kind of information and should be your first stop. Libraries have career guidance publications that describe the job duties, training requirements, working conditions, employment outlook, and earnings of different occupations. Reference librarians are very helpful, and computer data banks allow you to access a wealth of information quickly and easily.

Another great tool is *The Adams Jobs Almanac* (Bob Adams, Inc., 1994) which provides detailed information on over 10,000 employers in all major U.S. industries, including jobs commonly filled, experience required, benefits offered, and contact information. This comprehensive job search guide is updated annually and is available at your local bookstore.

There are many other resources at your disposal that should not be overlooked, including career centers, state employment service offices, guidance counselors, and trade unions and associations. Informational interviews are another great way to get the "insider's" view of your field of interest—and are an effective networking tool that could lead to job opportunities (see chapter 14 for more on informational interviews).

THE 20 HOTTEST CAREERS FOR WOMEN TODAY

Are you thinking about changing careers or moving up in your current field? Here is a list of hot professions that offer the best opportunities for women.

1. COMPUTER PROGRAMMER. About 317,000 more programmers will be needed in virtually every industry by the year 2005. Increasingly, employers are looking for programmers who are experienced in particular fields, such as accounting or biotechnology.

2. DATABASE MANAGER. Working for a broad spectrum of employers, database managers administer and control the data resources of an organization, ensuring security and recovering corrupted data. By 2005, openings are expected to grow by 25%.

3. LAN ADMINISTRATOR. The LAN (local area network) administrator determines how to integrate the needs of a department into a company's overall computer system. The number of LAN systems is expected to double from 2.4 million in 1992 to 4.1 million in 1996.

4. SYSTEMS ANALYST. Systems analysts work directly with management in analyzing, designing, or choosing the right application for a company's needs. Demand for these pros will increase 79% by 2005, making this one of the country's most in-demand occupations.

5. TELECOMMUNICATIONS MANAGER. Telecommunications managers oversee the information flow in and out of a company, through a network of telephones, fax machines, modems, voice mail, and teleconferencing. As businesses continue to go global, more telecommunications specialists will be increasingly in demand.

6. CROSS-CULTURAL TRAINER. These trainers help American businesses and expatriates understand and adjust to foreign cultures. As the U.S. economy goes global, these trainers will be ever more in demand.

7. EMPLOYEE TRAINER. These professionals determine employee's training needs, then develop classes and seminars for them in various areas. Corporations are expected to invest more and more time and money on worker training and education as the federal government increasingly focuses on this issue.

8. ENVIRONMENTAL CONSULTANT. Employers hire environmental consultants to inform them about the law, devise the best and least expensive method to dispose of hazardous waste materials and pollutants, and audit projects. The increased focus on environmental issues is likely to expand the environmental services sector by 60% in the next two years.

9. 50-PLUS MARKETER. America's growing older population, which is increasing by some 6,000 people every day, will increase demand for mature marketing experts.

10. SCHOOL ADMINISTRATOR. Some 62,000 educational administrators will be needed within the next 10 years as school enrollments rise and half of the nation's educational administrators retire.

11. FAMILY PHYSICIAN. While only 13% of doctors today are family doctors, new health care reforms may require as many as 50% of the doctor population to be primary-care physicians. This dearth of generalists is slowly driving salaries up and giving them a wide choice of areas in which to practice.

12. HOME HEALTH CARE NURSE. A recent survey found that 78% of Americans *prefer* home care, and the number of home health care agencies has mushroomed over the last 20 years, from 1,000 to 12,000. Home health care nurses will be needed to meet this demand.

13. MANAGED CARE MANAGER. Rising health care costs are creating demand at businesses and health care and insurance companies for managed care managers, who try to curtail costs while maintaining a standard of health care. This can be an ideal new career for former insurance agents.

14. NURSE PRACTITIONER. Working in nursing homes, clinics, hospitals, and private practice, nurse practitioners can provide, at lower costs, 60 to 80 percent of the primary and preventive care that was traditionally the doctor's domain. Although nurse practitioners constitute the second largest percentage of today's advanced-practice nurses, each still has at least three jobs waiting for her upon graduation.

15. PHYSICAL THERAPIST. The Bureau of Labor Statistics estimates that physical therapy is outgrowing every other health care occupation and will jump 76% by 2005. Graduating classes can't keep up with demand, and 15,400 jobs are currently unfilled.

16. DIVERSITY MANAGER. Working on company policies, diversity managers ensure that workers of assorted ages, races, and physical abilities are recruited and promoted. Corporate demand is considered "phenomenal" for diversity managers.

17. ENVIRONMENTAL MANAGER. Environmental managers integrate environmental considerations into everyday business decisions. Jobs in the waste-cleanup industry will increase by 16% over the next three years, thanks to heightened awareness and tougher enforcement.

18. HUMAN RESOURCES MANAGER. Layoffs, sexual harassment cases, affirmative-action programs, and the increasing complexity of workplace benefits have expanded the responsibilities and visibility of human resources managers. This field is estimated to grow by nearly a third over the next 12 years.

19. OMBUDSMAN. Currently used by about 500 corporations and 100 universities, these agents settle personal and professional rifts between employees and bosses.

20. PRODUCT MANAGER. Sometimes called a mini-CEO, this executive coordinates everything from research and development to marketing and monitoring sales of a particular product to ensure a healthy bottom line. The product development area improves and grows as more patents are being issued each year.

First appeared in *Working Woman* in July 1993. Written by Lois Anzelowitz. Reprinted with the permission of *Working Woman* magazine. Copyright ©1993 by *Working Woman* magazine.

Part II

Resumes and Cover Letters

3
Writing Your Resume

In today's competitive job market, companies often have hundreds of applicants for each job opening, but time to interview only a very small number of candidates. So an employer will have to reject most applicants after a brief skimming of their resumes. You could say that the resume is more the employer's tool for eliminating candidates than the candidate's tool for gaining consideration.

Unless you have phoned and talked to the employer—which you should do whenever you can—you will be chosen or rejected for an interview entirely on the basis of your resume and cover letter. Needless to say, they must be outstanding.

THREE BASIC TYPES OF RESUMES

There are three basic types of resumes. The chronological and functional resume formats are probably best known; the chrono-functional resume is a more recent innovation that combines the two basic resume formats.

The Chronological Resume

The chronological resume is actually a reverse chronological resume—items are listed in reverse chronological order, with your most recent schooling or job first. Names, dates, and places of employment are listed, and education and work experience are grouped separately.

This is the most common and readily accepted resume format. You should use a chronological resume if you have no large gaps in your work history and if your previous jobs relate to your current job objective. This format is a good choice for women moving up the career ladder.

The Functional Resume

A less common format is the functional resume. The functional resume focuses on the skills and talents you have developed and de-emphasizes job titles, employer names, and dates. The main purpose of a functional resume is to better the chances of candidates who might look weak on a chronological resume, or who are in the midst of a career change and wish to deflect attention from recent employment experience.

If you have skills and experience related to your job objective that are not highlighted by your employment history or if you have significant gaps in your employment history, the functional resume is best for you. This resume format is a good choice for first-time job seekers, including recent graduates and at-home moms and homemakers making the transition from home to the job market.

The Chrono-Functional Resume

The chrono-functional resume can be a powerful and flexible tool for the job seeker with a solid employment background and special skills she wants to emphasize. Like the chronological resume, it chronologically lists job history and education, while allowing the job seeker to highlight what makes her qualifications especially marketable.

This type of resume is a good choice for recent graduates with some job experience, career changers, and at-home moms and homemakers returning to the job market.

The following are samples of these resumes at their best. As you review these, consider which type of resume might be right for your job search.

Sample Chronological Resume

Joan Smith
178 Green Street
Washington, DC 20057
(202) 555-5555

EXPERIENCE

1985-present   UNIVERSITY OF VERMONT   BURLINGTON, VT

Associate Professor of Graphic Arts. Foster an atmosphere that encourages talented students to balance high-level creativity with emphasis on production. Instruct apprentices and students in both artistry and technical operations, including plate making, separations, color matching, background definition, printing, mechanicals, and color corrections. Instruction in black and white, and color.

1987-present   DESIGN GRAPHICS   BARRE, VT

Assistant Manager (part-time). Create silk screen overlays for a multitude of processes. Velo bind, GBC bind, perfect bind. Prepare posters, flyers, and personal stationery. Control quality, resolve printing problems, and meet or beat production deadlines. Work with customers to assure specifications are met and customers are satisfied.

EDUCATION

1982-1985 NEW ENGLAND SCHOOL OF ART AND DESIGN BOSTON, MA

Ph.D. in Graphic Design

1978-1982 UNIVERSITY OF MASSACHUSETTS   BOSTON, MA

B.A. in Art History, minor in Computer Science

AFFILIATIONS

Treasurer of Bookbuilders of Washington Society. Member of the National Association of Graphic Designers.

INTERESTS

Canoeing, volleyball, outdoor sports, photography.

REFERENCES

Available upon request.

Sample Functional Resume

Joan Smith
178 Green Street
Washington, DC 20057
(202) 555-5555

Summary
Solid background in plate making, separations, color matching, background definition, printing, mechanicals, color corrections, and supervision of personnel. A highly motivated manager and effective communicator. Proven ability to:

- Create commercial graphics
- Control quality
- Resolve printing problems
- Produce embossing drawings
- Color separate
- Analyze consumer acceptance

Qualifications
Printing: Black and white, and color. Can judge acceptability of color reproduction by comparing it with original. Can make four or five color corrections on all media. Have long developed ability to restyle already reproduced four-color art work. Can create perfect tone for black-and-white match fill-ins for resume cover letters.

Customer Relations: Work with customers to assure specifications are met and customers are satisfied. Can guide work through entire production process and strike a balance between technical printing capabilities and need for customer approval.

Management: Schedule work to meet deadlines. Direct staff in production procedures. Maintain quality control from inception of project through final approval for printing.

Specialties: Make silk screen overlays for a multitude of processes. Velo bind, GBC bind, perfect bind. Ability to prepare posters, flyers, and personal stationery.

Personnel Supervision: Foster an atmosphere that encourages highly talented artists to balance high-level creativity with a maximum of production. Meet or beat production deadlines. Instruct new employees, apprentices, and students in both artistry and technical operations.

Experience
Associate Professor of Graphic Arts, University of Vermont, Burlington, VT (1985-present).
Assistant Manager (part-time), Design Graphics, Barre, VT (1987-present).

Education
New England School of Art and Design, Ph.D. 1985
University of Massachusetts, B.A. 1982

Sample Chrono-Functional Resume

Joan Smith
178 Green Street
Washington, DC 20057
(202) 555-5555

QUALIFICATIONS
Solid background in plate making, separations, color matching, background definition, printing, mechanicals, color corrections, and supervision of personnel. A highly motivated manager and effective communicator. Proven ability to:

- Create commercial graphics
- Control quality
- Resolve printing problems

- Produce embossing drawings
- Color separate
- Analyze consumer acceptance

EXPERIENCE

UNIVERSITY OF VERMONT   BURLINGTON, VT
Associate Professor of Graphic Arts   **1985-present**

- Foster an atmosphere that encourages talented students to balance high-level creativity with emphasis on production.
- Instruct in both artistry and technical operations, including plate making, separations, color matching, background definition, printing, mechanicals, and color corrections.
- Instruct in black and white, and color.

DESIGN GRAPHICS   BARRE, VT
Assistant Manager (part-time)   **1987-present**

- Create silk screen overlays for a multitude of processes.
- Velo bind, GBC bind, perfect bind.
- Prepare posters, flyers, and personal stationery.
- Control quality, resolve printing problems, and meet or beat production deadlines.
- Work with customers to assure specifications are met and customers are satisfied.

EDUCATION

NEW ENGLAND SCHOOL OF ART AND DESIGN   BOSTON, MA
Ph.D., Graphic Design   **1985**

UNIVERSITY OF MASSACHUSETTS   BOSTON, MA
B.A., Art History   **1982**

AFFILIATIONS
Treasurer of Bookbuilders of Washington Society.
Member of the National Association of Graphic Designers.

No matter which resume format you choose, it's important to keep the following guidelines in mind while developing your personalized selling tool. These standard business tips will fare you well no matter what your profession, whether florist or financial consultant.

RESUME LENGTH

Unless you are applying for a top-level position, your resume should ideally fit onto a single page. If your resume is too long, you should consider trimming the content. Keep in mind that your resume is not meant to be a comprehensive, detailed history of your career, but a *summary* of your qualifications and skills.

> "What I'm looking for most [in a resume] is a clear-cut sense of career direction and momentum—or, at least, valid reasons why you made your job choices and changes. Don't assume, therefore, that if you dump a bunch of unorganized data on my desk, I'll fill in the gaps to make sense of your past. That's your job."
> —Douglas Richardson, Principal
> Richardson & Co.

PAPER SIZE

Use standard 8-1/2 x 11 inch paper. Employers handle hundreds of resumes; if yours is on a smaller sheet it is likely to be lost in the pile, and if it is oversized it may get crumpled and have trouble fitting in a company's files.

PAPER COLOR

White and ivory are the only acceptable paper colors for resumes and cover letters.

PAPER QUALITY

Standard, inexpensive office paper (20 pound bond) is generally acceptable for most positions. Executive and top-level positions may require more expensive stationery papers with a heavier weight or special grain.

TYPESETTING

Modern photocomposition typesetting gives you the clearest, sharpest image, a wide variety of type styles and effects such as italics, boldfacing, and book-like justified margins. In addition to being expensive, a typeset resume needs to be reset with every change.

> "I like wide margins, clean type (at least 10 or 12 point), clear headings, a logical format, bold and italic typeface that helps guide my eye, and selective use of bullets calling attention to important points."
> —Douglas Richardson, Principal
> Richardson & Co.

COMPUTERS, WORD PROCESSING, AND DESKTOP PUBLISHING

The most flexible way to prepare your resume is on a computer or word processor. This allows you to make changes almost instantly, and to store different drafts on disk. Word processing and desktop publishing systems also give you many different options that a typewriter does not, such as boldfacing for emphasis, different "fonts" or typefaces, and justified margins.

The end result, however, will be largely determined by the quality of the printer you use. A dot matrix printer is a poor choice for a resume because the type is much rougher than that of a typewriter. You need at least "letter quality" type. (Do not use a "near letter quality" printer.) Laser printers provide the best quality lettering from a computer.

TYPING

Household typewriters and office typewriters with nylon or other cloth ribbons are not acceptable for typing the resume you will have printed. If for some reason you decide against word processing or typesetting, hire a professional with a high-quality office typewriter with a plastic ribbon (usually called a "film ribbon").

PRINTING

Find the best quality offset printing process available. Do not make your copies on an office photocopier. Only the personnel office might see the resume you mail; everyone else might see only a copy of it. Copies of copies quickly become illegible. Some professionally maintained, very high-quality photocopiers are of adequate quality if you are in a rush, but top quality offset printing is best.

GUIDELINES FOR RESUME CONTENT

Here are some guidelines to help you construct resumes that practically shout "success!".

> "I like to see a summary of accomplishments and I routinely eliminate candidates whose objectives don't target the job opening."
> —David Palmer, Human Resource Director
> East New York Savings Bank

Be factual. In many companies, inaccurate information on a resume or other application will be grounds for dismissal as soon as the inaccuracy is discovered. Protect yourself.

Be positive. You are selling your skills and accomplishments in your resume. If you achieved something, say so, and put it in the best possible light. Don't hold back or be modest—no one else will. At the same time, however, don't exaggerate to the point of misrepresentation.

Be brief. Your resume will be scanned, not read. Short, concise phrases are much more effective than long-winded sentences. Consider the difference between these two examples:

Long-winded:
Over the course of the months of December 1993 and January 1994, I completely redid the inventory system at my place of employment, which ended up resulting in a final savings of a great deal of money—perhaps $10,000. It was also considerably easier to perform office tasks efficiently under the new arrangement, not only for myself, but also for others who worked with me at the store.

Clear and concise:
Winter, 1993: Designed and implemented new inventory system, resulting in a cost savings of approximately $10,000 and increased employee efficiency.

Emphasize relevant experience. Slant your past accomplishments toward the type of position that you hope to obtain. Do you hope to supervise people? If so, state how many people, performing what function, you have supervised. De-emphasize any positions that are irrelevant to your current job objective.

Stress your results. Elaborate on how you contributed to your past employers. Did you increase sales, reduce costs, improve a product, implement a new program? Were you promoted? *Do not simply list your responsibilities!*

ACTION VERBS make resumes come alive. Which are right for your resume?

accelerated	designed	innovated	recruited
accomplished	developed	instructed	regulated
achieved	devised	integrated	reorganized
administered	directed	interpreted	represented
advised	edited	launched	researched
analyzed	educated	maintained	resolved
appointed	encouraged	managed	restored
arranged	established	marketed	restructured
assisted	evaluated	mediated	retrieved
attained	examined	monitored	reviewed
balanced	executed	negotiated	revised
budgeted	expanded	operated	scheduled
built	expedited	organized	shaped
calculated	extracted	performed	sold
cataloged	facilitated	persuaded	solved
chaired	formulated	planned	streamlined
collaborated	founded	prepared	summarized
compiled	generated	presented	supervised
composed	headed	prioritized	taught
computed	helped	processed	trained
conducted	identified	produced	upgraded
constructed	illustrated	programmed	utilized
consulted	implemented	promoted	worked
created	improved	proposed	wrote
delegated	increased	provided	
demonstrated	initiated	published	

PROOFREADING IS ESSENTIAL

Whether you typed your resume yourself or paid to have it produced professionally, mistakes on resumes can be embarrassing, particularly when something critical (such as your name) is misspelled. No matter how much money you paid to have your resume written or typeset, you are the only one who will lose if there is a mistake. So proofread it as carefully as possible. Get a friend to help you—read your draft aloud as your friend checks the proof copy. Then have your friend read aloud while you check. Next, read it word by word, checking for spelling and punctuation.

If you are having your resume typed or typeset by a resume service or a printer, and you can't bring a friend or take the time during the day to proof it, pay for it and take it home. Proof it there and bring it back later to have it corrected and printed.

If you wrote your resume on a word processing program, use that program's built-in spelling checker to double-check for spelling errors. Most quality word processors include this convenient feature; however, a spelling checker is not a substitute for proofreading your resume—it must still be proofread to ensure that there are no errors. (Bear in mind that a spelling checker cannot flag errors such as "to" for "two," or "bills" for "skills.")

4
Special Scenario:
Students and Recent Graduates

Whether you're graduating from high school or college, those of you with little or no work history face the same dilemma: it's tough to get a job without experience and it seems to be impossible to gain experience without getting hired. But, as you will see, there are ways to get around this by emphasizing your strengths and educational achievements.

WHICH TYPE OF RESUME IS RIGHT FOR YOU?
The type of resume you should use really depends on your job experience. If you don't have any work history, you should use a functional resume format, emphasizing your strong points, such as:

1. Education. This should be your primary focus.
2. Special achievements. This could be almost anything from having an article published to graduating with honors.
3. Awards and competitive scholarships.
4. Classes, internships, theses, or special projects that relate to your job objective.
5. Computer knowledge. Are you familiar with a Mac or PC? What software programs do you know?
6. Language skills. Are you fluent in a foreign language? Be sure to indicate both written and verbal skills.
7. Volunteer work.
8. Committees and organizations.
9. Extracurricular activities.

If you have some work experience, such as a part-time job as the editor of your school paper, you should use the chrono-functional resume format. Recruiters like to see some kind of work history, even if it doesn't relate to your job objective, because it demonstrates that you have a good work ethic. However, it's also important to emphasize any special skills or qualifications you have, including the above information.

RESUME TIPS AND POINTERS

Your resume should fit onto one page and everything should be easy to find. Use bullets to highlight your most important skills, qualifications, and achievements. Unless you have more than two years of full-time work experience, you should emphasize your education most. You can accomplish this by listing your education at the top of your resume and by elaborating on special classes you took, achievements you made, and awards you received. You should try to avoid paragraphs longer than six lines; if necessary, rewrite the material into two or more paragraphs.

Including high school information is optional for college grads. If you have made exceptional achievements in college and in your summer or part-time jobs, you should omit your high school information. If you decide to include your high school achievements, describe them more briefly than your college achievements.

It's a good idea to use a brief, general job objective. This will give your resume focus while keeping all your opportunities open. A good job objective would be "A career in public relations" or "An entry-level position within an operations management environment."

If you have already graduated, you should begin "Awarded the degree of. . ." If you are still working on your degree, you should begin with the phrase "Candidate for the degree of . . ." If you did not graduate and are not currently pursuing your degree, you should simply list the dates you attended and the courses studied. For example, "Studied mathematics, physics, chemistry, and statistics." Never include a grade point average (GPA) under 3.0 on your resume. If your GPA in your major field of study is higher than your overall GPA, include it either in addition to or instead of your overall GPA.

When describing your work history, you should avoid simply listing your job duties. Focus on accomplishments and achievements, even if they are small. Consider the difference:

> *Weak:* "Lifeguard at busy public beach. Responsible for safety of bathers and cleanliness of the beach and parking areas."
>
> *Strong:* "Lifeguard at busy public beach. Established recycling program for bottles and cans."

Alternatively, if you have had many different jobs, you may choose to emphasize only two or three and list the rest under the heading "Other Experience" without individual job descriptions. For example:

> *Other Experience:* Floor and stockroom clerk at university bookstore, server, lifeguard, and courier.

Bear in mind that your resume is an advertisement for yourself, not an affidavit. Do not feel compelled to list every job you've ever had. Instead, focus on the positions you've had that relate to your current objective or that speak most positively of your experience.

You should list your personal interests and hobbies only if they are directly relevant to the type of job you are seeking. For instance, if you are applying to a company that greatly values teamwork, indicating the team sports you've played will probably be advantageous. When in doubt, however, leave it out.

Do not include your age, weight, height, marital status, race, religion, or any other personal information unless you feel that it directly pertains to the position you're seeking. For instance, marital status might be relevant if you are seeking a job working as a divorce counselor or writing for a singles magazine. Also, you should avoid listing references on your resume. This is most often viewed as inappropriate and unprofessional.

Although you will want to present yourself in the best possible light, always be truthful on your resume. More and more companies are checking resumes these days and false information is often considered grounds for dismissal, even years after you are hired. And don't forget to proofread for spelling errors and accuracy!

RECOMMENDED RESOURCES

The Complete Resume & Job Search Book for College Students by Bob Adams and Laura Morin (Bob Adams, Inc., 1992). Available at most bookstores.

Games Your Mother Never Taught You: Corporate Gamesmanship for Women by Betty Harragan (Warner Books, 1986). Available at most bookstores.

Knock 'em Dead: The Ultimate Job Seeker's Handbook by Martin Yate (Bob Adams, Inc., 1994). Available at most bookstores.

What Color is Your Parachute? by Richard Bolles (Ten Speed Press, 1994). Available at most bookstores.

Working Woman magazine. P.O. Box 3276, Harlan, IA 51593-2456. (800) 234-9675. Available at newsstands.

The Clairol Mentor Program ^{c}/$_o$ Clairol Inc., 345 Park Avenue, New York, NY 10154. Attention: Ellen Anderson.

National Association for Female Executives (NAFE), 30 Irving Place, New York, NY 10003. (800) 634-6233.

5
Special Scenario:
At-home Moms and Homemakers Entering the Job Market for the First Time

If you have little or no paid work experience, you may find yourself afflicted with self-doubt. Who would pay you to do what you know? But the fact is that skills are developed through all life experiences, not just through paid jobs and formal training. As you will see, you have all kinds of marketable skills and experience that you're probably overlooking—you know, the work you've been doing all these years and never got paid for? The trick here is to identify the job skills you have and match them with an employer's needs.

WHICH TYPE OF RESUME IS RIGHT FOR YOU?
The functional resume is perfect for your needs. It allows you to emphasize your special skills and qualifications while downplaying your lack of paid job experience.

FIRST, ASSESS YOUR SKILLS
Before you can write your resume, you'll need to determine exactly what your special skills and qualifications are. On a separate sheet of paper, list the activities you do on a regular basis. Be sure to include the following:

1. Special achievements. This could be almost anything, such as raising a family, planning a wedding, organizing a car pool, learning how to use a computer, coaching a soccer team, leading a Girl Scout troop, or organizing a community bake sale.
2. Classes you've taken. Have you taken a course in personal finance? A drawing class? Have you earned a degree?
3. Unique talents. Do you play the guitar? Do you throw pottery? Do you garden?
4. Computer knowledge. Do you create your household's budget on a particular system? Do you use a variety of software programs when organizing fund-rais-

ers, volunteering your services to your local church, or typing up the minutes from a local PTA meeting?

5. Specific job-related skills. Do you manage your household finances? If so, then you have accounting skills. Can you type, file, photocopy, fax, or answer telephones?

6. Language skills. Are you fluent in a foreign language? Can you write and read as well as speak it?

7. Volunteer work. For example, have you organized a charity bazaar or volunteered at a homeless shelter?

8. Committees and organizations. For instance, are you a member of the PTA or a neighborhood watch program?

9. Hobbies and areas of special interest. This could include almost anything, like sports, cooking, sewing, woodworking, or antique collecting.

You are probably beginning to recognize all the special skills you have. Now, on your list of activities, write down the specific skills, talents, and abilities required to perform these tasks. Which ones can be translated to a job outside the home? Where would they be most useful? For example, gardening requires creative, design, and visualization skills as well as a knowledge of agricultural concepts. These skills would be particularly valuable to florists, garden centers, and the produce department of your local grocery store.

> "During a job interview, Erma Bombeck told the personnel manager that she had been a wife and mother for all those years and needed extra sheets over and above those on the application form to list her background and skills. Needless to say, she got the job."
> —Charles Logue, Ph.D., author
> *Outplace Yourself: Secrets of an Executive Outplacement Counselor*

RESUME TIPS AND POINTERS

Your resume should fit onto one page and everything should be easy to find. Use bullets to highlight your most important skills, qualifications, and achievements. You should try to avoid paragraphs longer than six lines; if necessary, rewrite the material into two or more paragraphs.

It's a good idea to use a brief, general job objective. This will give your resume focus while keeping all your opportunities open. A good job objective would be "A career in public relations" or "An entry-level florist's position in a team-oriented, creative environment."

Tailor your resume to the specific job you're seeking. In other words, if you are seeking a job at a florist, your resume should emphasize your gardening skills; if you are applying for an accounting position, your resume should reflect your skills and experience in that area. This should be the most detailed part of your resume.

Be sure to include your education. What degrees have you earned? Have you taken any courses related to your job objective? If you have little or no education beyond high school, don't panic! Include the name of your high school, its location, and the year you graduated.

You should list your personal interests and hobbies only if they are directly relevant to the type of job you are seeking. For instance, if you are applying to a company that greatly values teamwork, including the fundraiser you organized with other neighborhood women will probably be advantageous. When in doubt, however, leave it out.

Do not include your age, weight, height, marital status, race, religion, or any other personal information unless you feel that it directly pertains to the position you're seeking. For instance, age might be relevant if you are seeking a job at a senior's organization that prefers its employees to be in a certain age range.

Always be truthful. Since you've already determined that you have many marketable skills, there's no need to exaggerate or make them up. Also, you should avoid listing references on your resume, which is often viewed as inappropriate and unprofessional. And don't forget to proofread for spelling errors and accuracy!

RECOMMENDED RESOURCES

Knock 'em Dead: The Ultimate Job Seeker's Handbook by Martin Yate (Bob Adams, Inc., 1994). Available at most bookstores.

Returning to the Job Market: A Woman's Guide to Employment Planning by the Work Force Programs Department (AARP, 1992). To order, write: AARP, 601 E Street NW, Washington, DC 20049.

What Color is Your Parachute? by Richard Bolles (Ten Speed Press, 1994). Available at most bookstores.

Working Woman magazine. P.O. Box 3276, Harlan, IA 51593-2456. (800) 234-9675. Available at newsstands.

National Association for Female Executives (NAFE), 30 Irving Place, New York, NY 10003. (800) 634-6233.

Women Work! The National Network for Women's Employment, 1625 K Street NW, Suite 300, Washington, DC 20006. (202) 467-6346.

6
Special Scenario:
At-home Moms Returning to the Job Market

There's no doubt about it, if you're a woman who's spent more time with her family re-
cently than in the work force, you're facing some troubling issues. You may be feeling anxious,
wondering if you still have what it takes to "make it" out there. The key element for you is to
make sure all of your skills are up-to-date. If they aren't, you should consider retraining, which
might mean learning a new computer program or taking a class at a local college. If your skills
are current, not to worry! What you'll need to emphasize on your resume is your previous job
experience and skills, ways you've kept up-to-date during your leave (reading trade journals,
doing free-lance work, attending seminars), and the skills you've learned at home that can be
transferred to the workplace. (See chapter 5 for more information about transferring skills from
home to the workplace.)

WHICH TYPE OF RESUME IS RIGHT FOR YOU?
The chrono-functional resume format works well for you, because it allows you to give primary emphasis to your qualifications and previous job experience while incorporating the
skills you've learned during your leave. Be sure to include:

1. Skills and qualifications specifically related to your job objective. These should
   be the primary focus of your resume.
2. Employment history. Include only the experience that relates to your current job
   objective. This should be the secondary focus of your resume.
3. Job-related awards and special recognition. For example, have you ever been
   named "Employee of the Month" or been recognized for achievement in your
   trade journal?

4. Special accomplishments you made at work. This could be almost anything such as winning a new account, installing a new computer system, cutting costs, establishing a work recycling program, or earning a promotion.
5. Accreditation, licenses, and certifications.
6. Degrees, course work, seminars, and job training.
7. Computer knowledge. Are you familiar with a particular computer system? What software programs do you know?
8. Any publishing credentials or patents awarded.
9. Professional organizations and associations you belong to.
10. Special achievements you've made during your leave. This could be almost anything, such as organizing a car pool, learning a new language, or coaching a soccer team.
11. Volunteer work. For example, have you organized a March of Dimes walkathon or volunteered at an abused women's shelter?

RESUME TIPS AND POINTERS

Your resume should fit onto one page and everything should be easy to find. Use bullets to highlight your most important skills, qualifications, and achievements. You should try to avoid paragraphs longer than six lines; if necessary, rewrite the material into two or more paragraphs.

You'll want to emphasize the progress you've made in your career. If you were promoted or took on additional responsibilities, say so. Do not, like so many mistaken job seekers, simply list the job duties for each position you've held. It's vitally important to focus on specific accomplishments and achievements, even if they are small. Consider the difference:

> *Weak:* "Responsibilities included serving as contact for brokerage firms, preparing financial reports, corresponding with shareholders, processing financial transaction requests, and training and supervising staff."

> *Strong:* "Served as principal contact for eight brokerage firms. Provided tax information to shareholders, prepared daily and monthly financial reports, and processed financial transaction requests. Trained and supervised staff of six. Implemented new computer system, resulting in a 30% increase in department efficiency."

Keep in mind as you list your job history that your resume is an advertisement for yourself, not an affidavit. Do not feel compelled to include every job you've ever had. Instead, focus on the positions you've had that relate to your current objective or speak most positively of your experience.

You should list your personal interests and hobbies only if they are directly relevant to the type of job you are seeking. For instance, if you are applying to a company that greatly values teamwork, including the fundraiser you organized with other neighborhood women will probably be advantageous. When in doubt, however, leave it out.

Do not include your age, weight, height, marital status, race, religion, or any other personal information unless you feel that it directly pertains to the position you're seeking. For instance, marital status might be relevant if you are seeking a job working as a divorce counselor or writing for a singles magazine. Also, you should avoid listing references on your resume. This is most often viewed as inappropriate and unprofessional.

Although you will want to present yourself in the best possible light, always be truthful on your resume. More and more companies are checking resumes these days and false information is often considered grounds for dismissal, even years after you are hired.

And don't forget to proofread for spelling errors and accuracy!

RECOMMENDED RESOURCES

Knock 'em Dead: The Ultimate Job Seeker's Handbook by Martin Yate (Bob Adams, Inc., 1994). Available at most bookstores.

Returning to the Job Market: A Woman's Guide to Employment Planning by the Work Force Programs Department (AARP, 1992). To order, write: AARP, 601 E Street NW, Washington, DC 20049.

What Color is Your Parachute? by Richard Bolles (Ten Speed Press, 1994). Available at most bookstores.

Working Woman magazine. P.O. Box 3276, Harlan, IA 51593-2456. (800) 234-9675. Available at newsstands.

National Association for Female Executives (NAFE), 30 Irving Place, New York, NY 10003. (800) 634-6233.

7

Special Scenario:
Career Changers

For those of you who have devoted your career exclusively to one profession or industry, work experience really isn't an issue. You have lots of experience . . . . but none of it relates to your current job objective. No problem! Instead of emphasizing your job history, you'll just have to emphasize the skills you've acquired that apply to the job your seeking. For example, let's say your career has been in real estate and, in your spare time, you like to run in marathons. Recently, you heard about an opening in the sales and marketing department at an athletic shoe manufacturer. What you need to do is emphasize the skills you have that the employer is looking for. Not only do you have strong sales experience, you're familiar with the needs of the company's market, and that's a powerful combination!

WHICH TYPE OF RESUME IS RIGHT FOR YOU?
The functional resume is perfect for your needs. It emphasizes your skills, not just your job history. Be sure to include:

1. Specific job skills that relate to your current job objective. This should be the primary focus of your resume.
2. Degrees, course work, seminars, and job training that relates to your current job objective.
3. Accreditation, licenses, and certifications relating to your current job objective.
4. Volunteer work relating to your current job objective.
5. Special accomplishments you've made that relate to your current job objective. This could be almost anything such as winning a lucrative account, implementing a new computer system, cutting costs, or establishing a work recycling program.
6. Awards and special recognition. For example, have you been named "Employee of the Month" or recognized for achievement by your trade association?
7. Professional organizations and associations.

> "If you can show an employer how your innate abilities and personality traits will benefit the company, you can win the position over other, more experienced candidates who don't know how to sell themselves."
>
> —Taunee Besson, President
> Career Dimensions

RESUME TIPS AND POINTERS

Your resume should fit onto one page and everything should be easy to find. Use bullets to highlight your most important skills, qualifications, and achievements. You should try to avoid paragraphs longer than six lines; if necessary, rewrite the material into two or more paragraphs.

Use a brief, general job objective. It will give your resume focus while keeping all your opportunities open. A good job objective would be "A career in broadcasting" or "A mid-level marketing position in a dynamic environment."

List personal interests and hobbies only if they are directly relevant to the type of job you are seeking. For instance, if you are applying to a company that greatly values teamwork, putting the team sports you've played on your resume will probably be advantageous. When in doubt, however, leave it out.

Do not include your age, weight, height, marital status, race, religion, or any other personal information unless you feel that it directly pertains to the position you're seeking. For instance, marital status might be relevant if you are seeking a job working as a divorce counselor or writing for a singles magazine. Also, you should avoid listing references on your resume. This is most often viewed as inappropriate and unprofessional.

Although you will want to present yourself in the best possible light, always be truthful on your resume. More and more companies are checking resumes these days and false information is often considered grounds for dismissal, even years after you are hired.

And don't forget to proofread for spelling errors and accuracy!

RECOMMENDED RESOURCES

Career Shifting: Starting Over in a Changing Economy by William Charland, Ph.D. Available at most bookstores. $9.95

Knock 'em Dead: The Ultimate Job Seeker's Handbook by Martin Yate (Bob Adams, Inc., 1994). Available at most bookstores.

What Color is Your Parachute? by Richard Bolles (Ten Speed Press, 1994). Available at most bookstores.

Working Woman magazine. P.O. Box 3276, Harlan, IA 51593-2456. (800) 234-9675. Available at newsstands.

National Association for Female Executives (NAFE), 30 Irving Place, New York, NY 10003. (800) 634-6233.

8

Special Scenario:
Women Moving Up the Career Ladder

So you're finally reaping the rewards for all the hard work and long hours you've been putting in. But now you don't want to lessen your opportunities with a resume that's weak or ineffective. Your resume needs to show all the progress you've made so far—that you're building a career, not doing a job. Your resume should practically shout "Success!"

WHICH TYPE OF RESUME IS RIGHT FOR YOU?

The chronological resume is best for your needs, because it shows the progress you've made in your career. Your job experience is the focus of your resume, whereas education and other elements are downplayed. You'll want to be sure to include the following:

1. Special accomplishments. This could be almost anything such as researching a long-distance phone plan that saved your company money, winning a new account, cutting costs, or earning a promotion.
2. Awards and special recognition. For example, have you been named "Salesperson of the Year" or recognized for always staying within your department's budget?
3. Specific job skills that relate to your objective.
4. Computer knowledge. Which computer systems and software programs are you familiar with?
5. Degrees, course work, seminars, and job training.
6. Accreditation, licenses, and certifications.
7. Publishing credentials and patents awarded.
8. Professional organizations and associations.

RESUME TIPS AND POINTERS

If you are seeking a top-level position, your resume should be two pages long. Otherwise, it should fit onto one page. Use bullets to highlight your most important skills, qualifications, and achievements. You should try to avoid paragraphs longer than six lines; if necessary, rewrite the material into two or more paragraphs.

You'll want to emphasize the progress you've made in your career, with primary focus on your current or most recent job. If you've been promoted or have taken on additional responsibilities, say so. Do not, like so many mistaken job seekers, simply list the job duties for each position you've held. It's vitally important to focus on specific accomplishments and achievements, even if they are small. Consider the difference:

> *Weak:* "Responsibilities included serving as contact for brokerage firms, preparing financial reports, corresponding with shareholders, processing financial transaction requests, and training and supervising staff."

> *Strong:* "Served as principal contact for eight brokerage firms. Provided tax information to shareholders, prepared daily and monthly financial reports, and processed financial transaction requests. Trained and supervised staff of six. Implemented new computer system, resulting in a 30% increase in department efficiency."

Keep in mind as you list your job history that your resume is an advertisement for yourself, not an affidavit. Do not feel compelled to include every job you've ever had. Instead, focus on the positions you've had that relate to your current objective or speak most positively of your experience.

Do not use a job objective. Presumably, your resume shows a strong career path, so that an objective is really unnecessary. Worse, it could eliminate you from consideration for other positions than the one for which you're applying.

List personal interests and hobbies only if they are directly relevant to the type of job you are seeking. For instance, if you are applying to a company that greatly values teamwork, including the team sports you've played on your resume will probably be advantageous. When in doubt, however, leave it out.

Do not include your age, weight, height, marital status, race, religion, or any other personal information unless you feel that it directly pertains to the position you're seeking. For instance, marital status might be relevant if you are seeking a job working as a divorce counselor. Also, you should avoid listing references on your resume. This is most often viewed as inappropriate and unprofessional.

Although you will want to present yourself in the best possible light, always be truthful on your resume. More and more companies are checking resumes these days and false information is often considered grounds for dismissal, even years after you are hired.

And don't forget to proofread for spelling errors and accuracy!

RECOMMENDED RESOURCES

Games Your Mother Never Taught You: Corporate Gamesmanship for Women by Betty Harragan (Warner Books, 1986). Available at most bookstores.

Knock 'em Dead: The Ultimate Job Seeker's Handbook by Martin Yate (Bob Adams, Inc., 1994). Available at most bookstores.

Working Woman magazine. P.O. Box 3276, Harlan, IA 51593-2456. (800) 234-9675. Available at newsstands.

9 to 5, National Association of Working Women, 614 Superior Avenue NW, Suite 852, Cleveland, OH 44113. (800) 522-0925.

American Business Women's Association, 9100 Ward Parkway, Kansas City, MO 64114. (816) 361-6621.

National Association for Female Executives (NAFE), 30 Irving Place, New York, NY 10003. (800) 634-6233.

9
Sample Resumes

This chapter includes 70 excellent sample resumes for women in many different career stages. Some are for women moving up the career ladder, college students, at-home moms returning to the job market, and career changers. Others are resumes for specific jobs. Use them as a guide for writing your own job-winning resumes.

RESUMES FOR SPECIAL SITUATIONS

50-plus Job Candidate

At-home Mom Returning to the Job Market (A)

At-home Mom Returning to the Job Market (B)

Career Changer (A)

Career Changer (B)

Career Changer (C)

Displaced Homemaker (A)

Displaced Homemaker (B)

Displaced Homemaker (C)

Displaced Homemaker (D)

Former Small Business Owner

Freelancer

Gaps in Employment History

Part-time Employment History

Physically Challenged

Short Employment History

Some College But No Degree

Temporary Employment History

Weak Educational Background

RESUMES FOR STUDENTS

Business Administration Major

Computer Science Major

Education Major

English Major

Mathematics Major

Psychology Major

Recent High School Grad

Recent Grad School Grad

RESUMES FOR WOMEN MOVING UP THE CAREER LADDER

Accountant

Account Manger

Accounts Receivable Clerk

Administrative Assistant

Advertising Coordinator

Applications Programmer

Architect

Associate Editor

Attorney

Bank Teller

Chemist

Civil Engineer

Customer Service Representative

Dental Hygienist

Desktop Publisher

Director of Human Resources

District Manager

Emergency Medical Technician

Graphic Artist/Designer

Interior Designer

Laboratory Assistant

LAN Administrator

Marketing Intern

Nurse

Office Manager

Paralegal

Photographer

Physical Therapist

Publicist

Public Relations

Real Estate Broker

Recruiter

Restaurant Manager

Retail Store Manager

Sales Assistant

Sales Manager

Social Worker

Special Needs Educator

Surgeon

Therapist

Travel Agent

Urban Planner

Vice-President

50-PLUS JOB CANDIDATE

JOAN SMITH
178 Green Street
Huntington, WV 25702
(304) 555-5555

OBJECTIVE:
A position in small plant management. Willing to relocate and/or travel.

SUMMARY OF QUALIFICATIONS:
More than thirty years of experience encompassing plant management to include sales, production, plant maintenance, systems, personnel, and related functions. Hired, trained, and supervised personnel. Additional experience as Sales Counselor in the educational field. Good background in customer relations and human resources.

CAREER HIGHLIGHTS:

The Westview Schools   Huntington, WV
<u>Career Counselor</u>   1981-Present
Contact and interview teenagers, young adults, and adults with reference to pursuing courses of higher education leading towards careers in a variety of business professions (secretarial, accounting, court reporting, business management, public relations, fashions and merchandising, computer and machine operating and programming, machine accounting, etc.). Administer aptitude tests to applicants and advise prospective students as to their aptitudes and best courses to pursue.

Greenbriar Corporation   Huntington, WV
<u>General Manager</u>   1972-1981
Assumed responsibility for management of this firm which originally employed twelve. Selected, set up, equipped, and staffed new facilities; hired, trained, and supervised skilled production personnel; set up incentive plans; quality production and cost controls; systems; plant maintenance; handled payroll, billing, credit and collection, purchasing, and finance.

Rosemont Inc.   Charleston, WV
<u>Assistant Plant Manager</u>, Laundry Company   1962-1972
Supervised all personnel in this plant which employed 250 people. Handled customer relations, complaints, quality control, and related functions.

EDUCATION:

Northeastern University, Boston, MA
Bachelor of Science degree
Industrial Relations and Accounting.

- Resume stresses Joan's extensive experience and significant accomplishments.
- Background summary accentuates Joan's acquired professional skills and impressive track record.

AT-HOME MOM RETURNING TO THE JOB MARKET (A)

JOAN SMITH
178 Green Street
Holland, MI 49423
(616) 555-5555

SUMMARY OF QUALIFICATIONS
- Excellent interpersonal and communication skills; cooperative, patient, supportive, and loyal team player.
- Highly adaptable and comfortable with unconventional/alternative settings and situations; familiar with academic, domestic, and creative routines and structures.
- Ability to ensure a project or task is completed accurately and in a timely fashion; strong on follow-up.
- Energetic and vital; remain active member of community organizations, while raising a large family.

EXPERIENCE

MICHIGAN HISTORICAL SOCIETY, Holland, MI   1992-Present
Researcher/Projects and Editorial Assistant - Part-time Volunteer
Research and work includes fact finding for the Michigan Tree Research Project; and a four-year study on In-depth Biographical History of Viking Presence in Early Michigan.

MICHIGAN MENTAL HEALTH CENTER, Detroit, MI   1991-Present
Co-Leader, Substance Abuse Program - Part-time Volunteer
Assist the Day Hospital staff with transition patients; assist on a team therapy program as well as in "modules" such as health awareness, gardening and literature groups.

HOLLAND PUBLIC WORKS DEPT.   Summers 1979 - Present
Activities Coordinator
Supervise local children in a variety of activities at the town playground; crafts, sports, games, etc. Requires knowledge of CPR and First Aid.

SHARONA REALTORS, Ypsilanti, MI   1978-79
Sales Representative

MICHIGAN STATE, East Lansing, MI   1976-78
Instructor, Art History
Developed curriculum; taught rudimentary aesthetics, method, and appreciation of modern American Art; monitored student progress, intervened where necessary.

EDUCATION

DETROIT SCHOOL OF PHOTOGRAPHY, Detroit, MI.   1982
Graduate, Applied Photography.

DREXEL, Philadelphia, PA. Bachelor and Master of Arts: History.   1976

- Resume focuses on Joan's past job experience while incorporating her functional qualifications.
- Volunteer work and community service lend strength to Joan's resume.

AT-HOME MOM RETURNING TO THE JOB MARKET (B)

Joan Smith
178 Green Street
Upper Montclair, NJ 07043
(201) 555-5555

CAREER OBJECTIVE
To utilize my extensive experience in nursing in a challenging position within the health care industry.

PROFESSIONAL EXPERIENCE
1988-92 MONTCLAIR MEMORIAL HOSPITAL, Montclair, NJ
R.N. Staff Nurse
Addictions Treatment Program
Patient care on 40-bed Mental Health Unit, assessing patients in crisis, interviewing and counseling, administering medication, Emergency Room consulting, collaborating with health care providers.
- Assess and evaluate patients with substance abuse problems.
- Responsible for the verification and pre-certification of insurance providers.
- Assess medical complications.
- Lead and co-lead educational groups for patients and their families.
- Collaborate with Treatment Team to implement in-patient and after care plans.

1985-88 **Staff Nurse/Psychiatric Addiction Emergency Service**
- Assessed of addicted and psychiatric patients to determine severity of illness and level of care needed.
- Collaborated with health care providers and medical team.

1983-85 MONMOUTH COLLEGE/NURSING PROGRAM, West Long Branch, NJ
Instructor/Medical Assisting Techniques
- Instructed students in the arts and skills of office medical procedures.
- Organized and planned curriculum, tested and graded students in written and practical methods.

1981-83 CITY OF NEWARK SCHOOL DEPARTMENT, Newark, NJ
Substitute School Nurse
- Administered first aid for students in K-12.
- Eye and ear testing, counseling and health teaching.

EDUCATION
JERSEY CITY HOSPITAL SCHOOL OF NURSING, Jersey City, NJ
Registered Nurse: Registration Number 10468, 1981

ACTIVITIES
Volunteer, Cedar Grove Nursing Home, 1993-present
Forward, Women's Soccer League, 1993-present

- Job objective gives resume focus without limiting Joan's opportunities.
- Personal interests and activities are relevant to Joan's field of interest.

CAREER CHANGER (A)

Joan Smith
178 Green Street
Decatur, GA 30032
(404) 555-5555

OBJECTIVE
To apply my seven years of experience with women's apparel, as well as my educational background, to a career in fashion design.

SUMMARY
- Area of expertise is creativity - from conception and design to marketing and sales.
- Self-starter attention to productivity and workmanship.
- Excellent communicator; adept at sizing up situations and developing new ideas or alternative courses of action in order to design, sell, or increase production.

QUALIFICATIONS
Design:
Conceptualized, coordinated, and designed in-store and window displays, including massive front window of major fashion center. Operated within a streamlined material budget appropriated by the manager, yet consistently generated award-winning window themes for $2.1 million department store.

Buying:
Attended fashion shows in New York, Milan, and Paris; assisted in the buying process. Perused fashion magazines on off-time; provided head buyer with information about upcoming styles.

EMPLOYMENT
DISPLAY COORDINATOR/ASSOCIATE BUYER, The Tudor Castle, Athens, GA 1989-1994

WINDOW DRESSER, Tanglewood's, Decatur, GA, 1987-1990

EDUCATION
Deverling School of Fashion Design, Decatur, GA
A.A. Fashion Design, 1994

REFERENCES
Available upon request.

- Functional format is ideal choice for career changers.
- Joan tailors her resume to her field of interest.

JOAN SMITH
178 Green Street
New Brunswick, NJ 08902
(201) 555-5555

OBJECTIVE:
Position in INTERNATIONAL CORPORATE RELATIONS which utilizes and challenges my business experience and knowledge of French Customs, Business Practices, and Language.

SUMMARY OF QUALIFICATIONS:

Communication:
Fluent in French, written and verbal. Knowledge of French culture and customs. Extensive Travel in France, Italy, and Germany.

Marketing:
Oversaw marketing, publications, and advertising for Travel Abroad Programs. Wrote and designed camera-ready ads, brochures, and flyers using desktop publishing system. Wrote, edited, and supervised production of departmental newsletter. Developed travel itineraries and budgets. Compiled and edited faculty brochure.

Administration:
Prepared departmental revenue and budget. Monitored registration progress. Processed faculty appointments and tenure reviews. Wrote minutes for administrative meetings. Office support for faculty members. Responsible for letters of appointment. Prepared exams and course/instructor evaluations. Assisted with registration and student inquiries.

Fundraising:
Worked on development proposals and College fundraising campaign. Organized special events.

EXPERIENCE:
RUTGERS UNIVERSITY, New Brunswick, NJ
Assistant to the Director, Foreign Language Department, June 1993-Present
Executive Secretary to the Dean, July 1992-May 1993
Faculty Secretary, September 1991-June 1992

EDUCATION:
RUTGERS UNIVERSITY, New Brunswick, NJ
BA in French Language and Culture Studies, 1991
Study Abroad Program, Paris, September 1989-August 1990

REFERENCES:
Furnished upon request.

- Joan's functional skills are highlighted while her unrelated work experience is de-emphasized.
- Joan's previous positions are listed without description under "Experience."

CAREER CHANGER (C)

Joan Smith
178 Green Street
Savannah, GA 31401
(912) 555-5555

OBJECTIVE:
To obtain an entry-level position in the publishing industry.

QUALIFICATIONS:

Editorial:
- Working knowledge of all aspects of the English language.
- Demonstrated copyediting and proofreading skills.
- Author of self-published book titled <u>Birding in the South</u>.
- First-hand knowledge of the book publishing industry.

Prepress:
- Supervise all aspects of book production.
- Assist with layout and formatting process.
- Prepare and organize art work for reproduction.
- Review and approve proofs.

Operations:
- Manage inventory control.
- Fill orders.
- Coordinate shipping and billing.

Promotion:
- Coordinate preparation and distribution of flier to bookstores.
- Design and place advertisement in <u>Publisher's Weekly</u>.
- Promote book at local book signing.

Computers:
- Thorough knowledge of Microsoft Word, Corel Ventura, Lotus 1-2-3, Excel, and Windows.

WORK EXPERIENCE:
1984- SAVANNAH SCHOOL DISTRICT, Savannah, GA
Present <u>Reading Specialist</u> (1991-Present), Implement the Publishing Center for Students.
<u>Coordinator/Teacher of the Gifted</u> (1988-1990), Advisor for school newspaper.
<u>Teacher, Fourth Grade</u> (1984-1987), Coordinated procedures for Writing Center.

EDUCATION:
College of Charleston, Charleston, SC
Bachelor of Arts in Elementary Education, May 1984.

- Joan's job objective is brief and to the point.
- Resume emphasizes qualifications pertaining to Joan's job objective.

DISPLACED HOMEMAKER (A)

JOAN SMITH
178 Green Street
Grenvil, NE 68941
(402) 555-5555

Objective:
An entry-level administrative position.

Summary of Qualifications:

ADMINISTRATION:
Accurate typing at 60 words per minute. Thoroughly experienced in all aspects of office administration, including record keeping, filing, and scheduling/planning.

ACCOUNTING:
Coordinate finances for a middle income family of five on a personal computer. Process accounts payable in a timely manner without compromising facets of the expenditure budget. Monitor checking account closely.

COMPUTERS:
Lotus 1-2-3, Microsoft Word, WordPerfect, IBM Compatible.

ORGANIZATION:
Organize a rotating carpool with five other mothers. Make several copies and distribute at least one month in advance.

Organize a monthly women's writing group concerned with reclaiming the feminine voice. Develop writing exercises that address the hidden spiritual elements in modern women's lives. Motivate members to channel stress, uncertainty, and fear into the gift of creativity. Act as mentor and friend.

LEADERSHIP:
President of Grenvil Historical Society, an organization of fifteen members concerned with educating public about Grenvil town history and preserving historic landmarks. Develop calendar of events; invite guest speakers, organize fundraising events. Provide meeting place, as well as materials and refreshments.

Coach a girls' soccer team, ages 7-11, in the Grenvil Youth Outreach Program (GYOR) from September to November. Provide players with the instruction, motivation, support, and outlook that will enable them to come away from each game with satisfaction and pride, no matter what the score.

Notable Accomplishments:
Organized fundraiser to renovate the Henry Wallace House; raised over $5,000. Several short stories published in regional literary magazines, including *The Loft*.

Education:
Grenvil Community College, Grenvil, NE
Courses in Creative Writing, Word Processing, and Accounting.

- Functional format is ideal for homemakers entering the job market for the first time.
- Resume emphasizes skills that can be transferred to the workplace.

DISPLACED HOMEMAKER (B)

JOAN SMITH
178 Green Street
Baton Rouge, LA 70807
(504) 555-5555

Objective:
To provide care in an adult home or child daycare environment.

Skills:
Care-Providing

- Provided care for a paraplegic in a private home setting for five years.
- Maintained a daily log of all medication administered.
- Coordinated a biweekly story hour at two local nursing homes.
- Delivered groceries to homebound seniors twice a week for two years.
- Administered medication.
- Acted as an assistant to seniors in wheelchairs through private and public transportation.

Communication

- Organized the care of an elderly relative within a nursing home for three years.
- Bargained with contractors about the adaptation of private homes for special needs adults.
- Provided counseling to the elderly, clarifying their wants and needs.
- Improved communication with support services for an elderly couple in order to improve their quality of life.
- Organized a pet visiting hour by acting as a liaison between two nursing homes and the local animal shelter.

Planning

- Organized day trips to local museums, parks, and shopping centers.
- Developed calendar of monthly in house events for two nursing homes.
- Planned biweekly shopping lists for several elderly individuals according to their physicians' specifications.
- Organized successful "Friend in Deed" program in which mobile seniors visited the homes of their house-bound peers.

Education:
Lexington High School, Lexington, KY

- Resume is geared specifically toward Joan's job objective.
- Joan's many achievements are emphasized.

DISPLACED HOMEMAKER (C)

JOAN SMITH

178 Green Street
Cheyenne, WY 82009
(307) 555-5555

Objective:
A position in Food Service in the public school system.

Related Experience:

Jameson Homeless Shelter   Cheyenne, WY
Weekday server. Act as a liaison between homeless and a national food distributor, securing special requests and unanimously favored items.

St. Bernadette's Parish   Cheyenne, WY
Coordinate annual bake sale; provide approximately ten percent of the bakery items sold.

Brady Family   Cheyenne, WY
Act as live-in nanny for eight-year old twin boys; duties include the preparation of their meals and snacks on a regular basis.

Lion's Club Carnival   Cheyenne, WY
Work the concession booths at annual carnival each June; prepare and serve such items as fried dough, sweet sausage, pizza, and caramel apples; maintain a receipt record of profits for event administrators.
Conduct informal cooking classes out of the Payne Community Center kitchen on a weekly basis.

Awards:
Award-winning country style cook.
Placed first in national fruit-based pie competition.
Won cash prize for best pot roast recipe, Reader's Digest.

Education:
Cheyenne Community College, Cheyenne, WY
Associates Degree, Home Economics

Interests:
Gourmet cook, Little League softball coach, avid gardener

References:
Available upon request

- Awards heading draws attention to Joan's significant accomplishments.
- Personal interests can provide a great topic for conversation during a job interview.

DISPLACED HOMEMAKER (D)

JOAN SMITH
178 Green Street
Stoneham, MA 02180
(617) 555-5555

Objective:
To secure a position as a management trainee

Summary of Skills:
Administration
- Led meetings of fifteen participants
- Created tentative plans for the quarterly meetings
- Supervised team of seven volunteer firefighters
- Scheduled musicians for the Bang's community center during the summer music festival
- Coordinated weekly films for "Culture on the Common" program during one summer
- Kept receipt records for yearly Exotic Foods Fest with revenue in excess of $50,000

Communication
- Developed grant requests for team of volunteer firefighters
- Led Christian youth group weekend retreats each month
- Tutored teenagers with math anxiety
- Spoke before groups of concerned teachers, parents, and citizens regarding adolescent violence
- Conducted telephone surveys assessing the overall happiness of teenagers with the local school system

Planning
- Coordinated youth group travel plans
- Planned calendar of events for recently opened teen center
- Developed new feedback oriented lesson plans for high school classrooms

Education:
>Massasoit Junior College, Canton, MA
>A.S. Management, 1978
>Honor society

Computer Skills:
>Lotus 1-2-3, Microsoft Word

Interests:
>Hiking, camping, and antique collecting

References:
>Available upon request

- Functional format focuses attention on Joan's major skills and accomplishments.
- Strong action verbs bring Joan's resume to life.

Joan Smith
178 Green Street
Clarksville, TN 37044
(615) 555-5555

OBJECTIVE
A challenging position in the field of sales and electronic publishing.

SUMMARY OF QUALIFICATIONS

- More than fifteen years of Art Director/Buyer and graphics/design production experience in the publishing field; extensive knowledge of type and mechanical preparation, budgeting and scheduling.
- Excellent interpersonal, communication, and managerial skills; adept at coordinating and motivating creative artists to peak efficiency.
- Aware of cost management and quality control importance on all levels.
- Self-motivated; able to set effective priorities and meet impossible deadlines.
- Productive in fast-paced, high-pressure atmosphere.

PROFESSIONAL EXPERIENCE
1978-1994   NO CONTEST GRAPHICS, Nashville, TN
Owner/President, Art Director/Buyer
Coordinate operations, 12-member production staff, freelance desktop publishers and illustrators. Maintain overview of works-in-progress to produce at optimum efficiency. Provide/advice to personnel in designing materials to appropriately meet client needs; conceptualize product; delegate staff to make decisions. Commission freelance agents by utilizing nationwide illustrator four-color manuscripts using watercolor illustrations, photography, or graphics. Act as liaison between executive personnel and staff. Budget each project; motivate artistic staff and typesetters to meet projected deadlines and remain within cost-efficient parameters. Projects include: greeting cards, care package kits, magazine fragrance inserts, cereal boxes, toy packages, coloring books (cover and contents), holographic bumper stickers, and retail store signs and logos.

1976-1978   NEW JERSEY LITHOGRAPH, Newark, NJ
Head of Typesetting & Design Department
Supervised staff in design and execution of print materials for commercial printer.

EDUCATION
CENTENARY COLLEGE, Hackettstown, NJ
A.S. in Technical Illustration, 1977

ART INSTITUTE OF NEWARK, Newark, NJ
Certified in Graphic Design, 1975

- Resume format is neat and professional.
- Attention-getting resume focuses on accomplishments and uses dynamic language.

FREELANCER

Joan Smith
178 Green Street
Richmond, VA 23294
(804) 555-5555

SUMMARY
Freelance writer and editor specializing in children's textbooks.

EXPERIENCE

Freelance Writer   1991-Present
Ben Curtis and Company: Gifted Child Program, grades 7-12
Tallvia Kincaide, Inc.: Writing Handbooks, grades 7-9
Jean K. Simmons Company: Ancient Civilizations Textbook, grade 12
Jean K. Simmons Press: Literature Program, grades 9-12
Create original manuscripts for student textbooks, annotated teacher's editions, and
numerous ancillaries. Materials include the following: teaching apparatus; questions
for responding, analyzing, and interpreting; thinking, writing, language, and
vocabulary exercises and worksheets; multi-page writing workshops; end-of-unit
features for writing and language skills; and collaborative learning activities. Design
prototypes for textbook and ancillary features. Conduct multicultural literature
searches.

Senior Editor, Secondary English, Jean K. Simmons Press   1986-1991
Project supervisor for Teacher's Editions of a composition and grammar program,
levels 6-9. Edited author manuscript for "Writing is Fun," level 7 & 8. Wrote
manuscript for "Writing is Fun," levels 9, 10, 11, and 12, including instruction, model
paragraphs, and assignments. Developed content and approach for units on critical
thinking and word processor use.

Editor, Secondary English, Educational Press   1984-1986
Project supervisor for Teacher's Editions and Teacher's Resource Masters of
vocabulary program, levels 9-12. Edited author manuscript for four levels of pupil
books for vocabulary program. Wrote exercises, reading comprehension passages,
and activities to support instruction. Conducted writing workshops for teachers as
follow-up to sales.

Associate Editor, Secondary English, Educational Press   1982-1984
Developed explanatory material and features for teacher's editions for grammar and
composition program, levels 9-12. Contributed to the development of vocabulary
program, including writing, editing, and selecting appropriate art.

EDUCATION

Clark University, Worcester, MA. Master of Arts, Education   1982
Boston College, Chestnut Hill, MA. Bachelor of Arts, English   1980

REFERENCES
Available upon request.

- Joan's clients are listed in italics followed by a general list of her duties and accomplishments.
- Resume emphasizes Joan's strong work history.

GAPS IN EMPLOYMENT HISTORY

JOAN SMITH
178 Green Street
Sumter, SC 29150
(803) 555-5555

Objective:
An editing position within a major publishing house.

Summary of Qualifications:
- More than seven years of writing/editing experience.
- Adept at managing multiple responsibilities simultaneously.
- Experienced at delegating authority and motivating others to ensure efficiency and productivity.
- Computer knowledge includes Lotus 1-2-3, Microsoft Word, WordPerfect, Pagemaker, and DOS.

Work Experience:

Editor-in-Chief, Renegade Magazine
Sumter, SC
Selected submissions, edited and wrote headlines for submissions and columns, laid out page, recruited columnists, trained associates from 1990-1993. Frequent copy editing and research.

Associate Editor, Modern Daze Magazine
New York, NY
Wrote articles for both the magazine and its associated newsletter, *Disembodied Voices*. Edited features and department articles from 1984-1988. Read and critiqued assigned articles from contributing editors.

Copy Editor, Heathcliff's Garden Magazine
Boston, MA
Edited news stories, wrote headlines, assisted with layout of page, occasionally solicited advertising, and helped with distribution from 1980-1982.

Other Experience:
Writer, professional musician, world traveler.
(Details available upon request.)

Military:
Army Corporal (honorable discharge).

Education:
University of Richmond, Richmond, VA
Bachelor of Arts, English, 1978
Le Student Roma, Rome, Italy
Intensive study of Italian language and culture, 1991

- Joan's obscures the gaps in her employment history placing dates of employ in her job descriptions.
- Functional format is another good option for candidates with gaps in employment history.

JOAN SMITH
178 Green Street
Johnson, VT 05656
(802) 555-5555

OBJECTIVE
To join a dynamic sales staff with a firm that has a need for a highly motivated representative skilled in retail markets.

SUMMARY OF PROFESSIONAL EXPERIENCE
- Four years of substantial experience in positions as Sales Representative, Retail Sales Manager, and Warehouse Manager with retail and a major wholesale organization.
- Assumed responsibility for divisional sales from $1.4 million to $2.1 million within one year.
- Hands-on experience in sales, inventory control, and promotion of chemicals, furniture, clothing, and seasonal products.
- Skilled in developing special merchandising effects to increase product visibility and sales.

WORK HISTORY

Raintree, Inc.
Seasonal Specialty Stores, Raintree Industries, Johnson, VT
Retail Manager (Part-time)   (1993-Present)
- Hire, train, schedule and supervise a highly productive staff of 11 selling and promoting a diverse product mix.
- Develop, implement, and expand seasonal merchandise and presentations for year-round sales. Greatly expanded product knowledge and sales through use of in store video and other image equipment.
- Select and purchase all billiard equipment and accessories.
- Prepare inventory projections, work on sales promotions (in-store and chain-wide). Excellent consumer base resulting in strong repeat business.
- Maintain financial control of all debits/credits.

Wholesale Warehouse Manager, (Part-time)   (1992-1993)
- Supervised a staff of 6 and controlled all aspects of shipping and receiving. Directed fleet scheduling maintenance as well as building maintenance control and security for this facility.

Sales Representative (Part-time)   (1991-1992)
- Increased all aspects of wholesale pool and supply and accessory business. Control of expanding sales and sales force. Established new sales and accounts within the New England area.

EDUCATION

Cornell University, Ithaca, NY
B.A. Business Administration, 1991.

- Part-time experience may be treated like full-time experience on a resume.
- Statistics and dollar figures quantify Joan's accomplishments.

PHYSICALLY CHALLENGED

JOAN SMITH
178 Green Street
Casper, WY 82604
(307) 555-5555

OBJECTIVE
An Engineering position in the field of Electro-Optics.

WORK EXPERIENCE

1993- JT Technology   Casper, WY
Present **ASSISTANT ENGINEER**

- Provide engineering support to various sensor and electro-mechanical areas.
- Solve engineering-related problems for production department; assist through direct observation, positive communication and dynamic interaction between production floor and test engineering management.
- Perform equipment and component testing; troubleshoot malfunctions; assist engineers with special projects and with department support tasks as required.
- Monitor current developments in the engineering fields for possible practical applications.

1990-1993 Charles Technology Corporation   Casper, WY
ASSISTANT ENGINEER

- Supervised various test engineering projects which required operating specialized equipment, documenting test results and making reports of findings to engineering management.
- Implemented software/hardware modifications and engineering changes requested by company clients.
- Assisted senior engineers with projects and performed support duties as needed.

1988-1990 Dishwashers, Etc.   Green Bay, WI
APPLIANCE TECHNICIAN

- Made household and commercial service calls to troubleshoot malfunctions, repair and/or replace various appliances.
- Installed new equipment; interacted with customers and coworkers in a pleasant and efficient manner.

EDUCATION

Associates of Science Degree in Electronic Technology, 1990
Green Bay Community College, Green Bay, WI
GPA 3.5/4.0

ACTIVITIES

New York Marathon
Placed 5th, Wheelchair Division - 1993

- Education is listed towards bottom of resume because Joan's practical experience outweighs her degree.
- Resume emphasizes Joan's contributions and achievements and the problems she has solved throughout her career.

SHORT EMPLOYMENT HISTORY

JOAN SMITH
178 Green Street
Kenosha, WI 53141
(414) 555-5555

Objective
A position within the operations department of a reputed brokerage firm.

Summary of Qualifications
- Detail-oriented; establish effective priorities.
- Able to implement decisions and expedite work flow to meet deadlines.
- Comfortable providing unlimited support during times of high pressure and stress.

Experience
KASS AND SON, INC., Kenosha, WI
Operations and Process Clerk (1994-Present)
- Open, log, reconcile, and verify new accounts.
- Reconcile daily customer service/new accounts input against computer printouts. Research/correct problems.
- Maintain/update files.
- Handle high-volume mailings to welcome new clients and initial mailing of Electronic Funds Transfer forms/letters.
- Recommend procedural changes to facilitate work flow.
- Interact with branch representatives.
- Assist with special projects as required including bookkeeping, handling President's incoming calls, and responding directly to customer inquiries.
- Converted manual check processing to electronic function.
- Eliminated major filing backlog.

Other Experience
Camp Teutonahwa, Butte, MT
Administrative Assistant (Part-time)
Billings Middle School, Billings, MT
Administrative Assistant (Part-time)

Volunteer Work
Jewish Education Association, Kenosha, WI
Resource Coordinator
Barbara Walsh Soup Kitchens, Bozeman, MT
Kitchen Worker/Shelter Coordinator

Education
WIDENER UNIVERSITY, Chester, PA
B.A. Management, 1988
President of Class, 1986-88
Formed Widener Chapter of Y.B.P.A. (Young Business People of America).
Membership began at 15 students; by 1993, it had swelled to 174.

- Impressive qualifications and volunteer and educational experience help to compensate for Joan's short employment history.
- Resume accentuates Joan's relevant experience; her unrelated jobs are listed under "Other Experience."

SOME COLLEGE BUT NO DEGREE

Joan Smith
178 Green Street
Dahlonega, CA 31597
(404) 555-5555

PROFESSIONAL OBJECTIVE
A challenging career continuation as an Accounting Assistant.

SUPPORTIVE QUALIFICATIONS
- Eight years experience and broad-based knowledge of the accounting field.
- Proficient with Lotus 1-2-3 Spreadsheets; general ledger, accounts receivable and payable, auditing and cash flow functions.
- Strong numerical and administrative abilities.
- Experience training incoming personnel.

HIGHLIGHTS OF PROFESSIONAL EXPERIENCE

1990-Present SAVANNA COMPTROLLER'S OFFICE, Dahlonega, CA
Accounting Assistant
- Monitor funding and financial reporting associated with various federal sponsors.
- Perform internal cost audits of terminated research contracts and grants.
- Coordinate audit and cash flow functions between CAO and other university departments.
- Audit and create financial reports, monthly/quarterly reports, government requirements and correspondence.

1987-1990 NOSTRADAMUS CORPORATION, Dahlonega, CA
Accounting Assistant
- Held complete responsibility for all receivables and payables.
- Implemented CRT operations; computerized financial reports and auditing.
- Strong telephone and personal contact in customer service and problem solving with purchasing department.
- Maintained computer master files and related input data.

EDUCATION

CREIGHTON UNIVERSITY, Omaha, NE
Course work in accounting, statistics, corporate finance, business law, and computers, 1985-1987.

PERSONAL INTERESTS

Photography * Tennis * Marathon Running

- Although Joan did not earn a degree, she lists relevant courses she took.
- Supportive qualifications illustrate Joan's key credentials.

JOAN SMITH
178 Green Street
Raleigh, NC 27611
(919) 555-5555

OBJECTIVE:
A long-term position in administration.

SKILLS & QUALIFICATIONS:
- Five years Accounting, Financial and Administrative experience.
- Computer knowledge includes IBM, Apple, and Honeywell.
- Outstanding communications and organizational skills.

EXPERIENCE:

11/94-Present   CARMICHAEL ENTERPRISES, Raleigh, NC
Accounting Clerk/Data Entry
Temporary Position
Prepare and maintain all general ledger accounts, records, and files. Input data on various computer systems, including IBM, Apple, and Honeywell.

6/94-10/94   CHAVEZ INVESTMENTS, Winston-Salem, NC
Customer Service Representative
Temporary Position
Responded to questions and assisted shareholders in regards to their stocks, bonds, equity and money market accounts, as well as tax questions. Approved check disbursements and utilized IBM computer system.

11/93-6-94   JOHN HANCOCK LIFE INSURANCE CO., Boston, MA
Purchasing Clerk
Temporary Position
Maintained general supply inventory levels and purchased general supplies and specially requested items and materials. Negotiated price and coordinated delivery with various vendors. Prepared purchase orders. Assisted in other administrative activities.

4/88-12/92   SCANLON CORPORATION, Chapel Hill, NC
Residential Counselor
Assisted and counseled mentally retarded and emotionally disabled adults in reading, math, personal hygiene, and motor skills.

OTHER EXPERIENCE:
Other temporary assignments have included: Receptionist, Order Entry Clerk, Switchboard Operator, Proofreader.

EDUCATION:
Clydeston Business School Certification, 1992
Kennedy High School Graduate, 1988

- Long-term temporary assignments may be treated like full-time permanent positions on a resume.
- Short-term assignments are listed under "Other Experience."

WEAK EDUCATIONAL BACKGROUND

Joan Smith
178 Green Street
Troy, MI 48098
(313) 555-5555

OBJECTIVE:
To fully utilize over ten years of experience in investment accounting within an allied field.

SUMMARY:
Experience in monitoring money flow in money market funds and mutual funds, as well as calculating the yield for various money market accounts, and pricing mutual funds.

EXPERIENCE:

GERGEW SERVICE COMPANY   Troy, MI
Senior Money Market Accountant   1989-Present
Determined daily available cash, calculated daily yields and dividends. Posted general ledger. RECONCILED trial balance accounts. Acted as liaison between fund traders and custodian banks. Prepared audit schedules. Assisted in training new personnel. Used both P.C. and CRT.

Mutual Fund Accountant   1986-89
Functions included daily pricing of common stock and bond funds, accruing and reconciling interest and dividend accounts, reconciling trial balance accounts and daily contact with brokers to obtain stock and bond quotes.

TIMBERCREST COMPANY,   Boston, MA
Assistant Supervisor   1985-86
Prepared schedules for fund audits. Prepared reports for fund managers. Assisted fund accountants with month-end trial balance reconciliation. Trained new personnel.

Fund Accountant   1983-85
Manually priced funds and posted journals and ledgers through trial balance. Heavy daily contact with brokers.

OTHER QUALIFICATIONS:
LICENSED MICHIGAN REAL ESTATE BROKER, 1982

EDUCATION:
Waterford High School, Waterford, MI
Graduated 1981

- Summary is concise and adds punch to resume.
- Joan's work experience is emphasized, while her limited education is de-emphasized.

BUSINESS ADMINISTRATION MAJOR

JOAN SMITH
409 Birch Road
Peru, Nebraska 68492
(402) 555-5555

Education

1991-present | UNIVERSITY OF NEBRASKA   LINCOLN, NEBRASKA
Candidate for the degree of Bachelor of Science in Business Administration, to be awarded in May 1995. Courses include Marketing, Statistics, Calculus, and Computer Applications. 3.8 grade point average in major, 3.6 overall grade point average.

President of National Honor Society in Business Administration. Dean's List all semesters. Varsity letter in tennis.

Internship

summer 1994 | KEYBROOK INVESTOR RESOURCE CENTER LINCOLN, NEBRASKA
Junior Client Service Representative. Served as principal contact for various brokerage firms. Trained and checked work of six other staff members. Provided tax information to shareholders, prepared daily and monthly financial reports, handled correspondence with shareholders, and processed financial transaction requests.

Experience

summers 1992-1993 | SUPER COMPUTER STORE   LINCOLN, NEBRASKA
Sales Associate for large computer store chain. Advised customers on a variety of computer software. Cashier and quality control. Promoted to Stock Person.

summer 1991 | BIG X DRUGSTORE   PERU, NEBRASKA
Merchandiser. Checked stock in, took inventory. Operated cash register.

part-time 1992-present | UNIVERSITY OF NEBRASKA   LINCOLN, NEBRASKA
Archival Research Assistant. Catalogued and reproduced documents and photographs and archival collection, cleaned and repaired damaged documents, transcribed oral history projects, located and acquired historic material, and coordinated with local archival organizations.

Skills Familiar with Lotus 1-2-3, Microsoft Word, and GW Basic.

References Available on Request

- Joan's job descriptions are short, concise, and effective. This resume will likely be examined more carefully than a long-winded one.
- Joan's internship bolsters her otherwise limited work experience.

COMPUTER SCIENCE MAJOR

Joan Smith
2 Graham Street
Grove City, Pennsylvania 16126
(412) 555-5555

EDUCATION

Gettysburg College   Gettysburg, Pennsylvania
Awarded a Bachelor of Sciences Degree in Computer Science with a Concentration in Programming. Key courses include Computer Organization & Architecture, Logic Design and Switching Theory, Discrete Mathematical Structures I-II, Data Structures and Algorithms, Operating Systems and Computer Networks, and Software Engineering. 3.65 grade point average. Graduated Summa Cum Laude in May 1995.

Member of Gettysburg Society of Computer Programmers. Tutor for introductory computer science courses. Member and competitor in Cycling Club.

WORK EXPERIENCE

PC Systems, Inc.   Philadelphia, Pennsylvania
Applications Programmer   Summer 1994
Wrote business-related software, including programs used for inventory control and order processing using COBOL. Tested finished programs for bugs and corrected them if they occurred.

Gettysburg College Computer Center   Gettysburg, Pennsylvania
Computer Lab Assistant   Part-time 1992-1994
Assisted students with software, hardware, and printing questions and problems. Trained students and faculty how to use word processing, database, spreadsheet, and desk-top publishing programs. Maintained and repaired equipment.

SOFTWARE

COBOL	dBase	Fortran	Lotus 1-2-3
Pascal	Unix Shell	Rexx	PageMaker
Assembly	Refal-5	WordPerfect	Microsoft Excel

HARDWARE

IBM 4341, 370VM/CMS, PC-XT, AT&T 3B2, AT, Mac SE, Mac 2E, Mac FX

REFERENCES

Available upon request.

- Joan's education is listed at the top of resume because it is her strongest qualification.
- Joan's impressive grade point average is listed under education; a GPA under 3.0 should not be included on a resume.

EDUCATION MAJOR

Joan Smith

School Address	**Permanent Address**
178 Green Street	23 Blue Street
Dayton, OH 45469	Oakwood, OH 45873
(513) 555-5555	(419) 444-4444

EDUCATION

University of Dayton   **Dayton, OH**
Bachelor of Arts Degree, Summa Cum Laude, May 1994
G.P.A.: 3.6/4.0 Dean's List, First Honors
Majors: Secondary Education, English

HONORS

Selected to speak at Commencement ceremonies
National Education Award, 1992
National Dean's List, 1990-1991, 1991-1992, 1993-1994
Who's Who Among Students, 1991,1992

ACTIVITIES

Student Admissions Program
Peer Advisement Program
Freshmen Assistance Program
School of Education Senate
Student Representative to Educational Policy Committee

EXPERIENCE

Spring **Substitute Teaching**   **Oakwood High School, Oakwood, OH**
1994 Work as substitute teacher in various disciplines for students in grades 7-12.

Fall 1993 **Student Teaching Full-Time Practicum   Kerrigan High, Kerrigan, OH**
Travel to site daily and assume full teaching responsibility for two junior accelerated American Literature classes and one freshman fundamental English class. Prepare, lecture, discuss, and evaluate units in literature and writing. Design and present lessons on Puritan writers, focusing on Nathaniel Hawthorne's *Scarlet Letter*. Provide writing instruction for paragraphs and essays.

Fall 1992 **Student Teaching Field Pre-Practicum Central High School, Dayton, OH**

Spring **Kerrigan High School**   **Kerrigan, OH**
1992 Visit site weekly to observe classes and gain practical teaching experience.

REFERENCES

Available upon request.

- Teaching practicums are an essential aspect of an education major's resume.
- Special honors indicate Joan's potential to excel.

ENGLISH MAJOR

Joan Smith
178 Green Street
Columbia, MO 65201
(314) 555-5555

OBJECTIVE
To contribute developed skills to a challenging position in the publishing field.

SUMMARY OF QUALIFICATIONS
- Four years publishing experience.
- Completely bilingual in English and Spanish; some knowledge of French.
- Extensive computer experience (formerly a Computer Science major): IBM, Macintosh, Compu-graphics, VAX.
- Proven writing skills; authored hundreds of pages of fiction in the past three years.
- Excellent communication abilities; lectured to a wide variety of audiences in a museum setting.

EDUCATION
DOWLING COLLEGE, Oakdale, NY
B.A., English, magna cum laude, May, 1994

COLLEGE ACTIVITIES
Plume, Literary Magazine   Fall 1990-Spring 1994
Editor (from Spring 1992), **Production and Business Coordinator**
Responsible for composing magazine budget and arranging specifications with printers.

Free-Lance Writer   Spring 1991-Spring 1994
Published book and movie reviews, essays, and short stories on different campus publications.

Dowling College Pictures   Spring 1992
Founding Member/Screenwriter
Wrote short movie production.

WORK EXPERIENCE
The Damien House Museum, Oakdale, NY   Spring 1994
Museum Assistant
Interpreted exhibits for visitors. Prepared/delivered short talks on historical subjects. Participated in organization of creative educational programs.

Bindings Bookstore, Oakdale, NY   Fall 1992
Sales Clerk/Floor Person
Maintained stock; helped customers make selections; registered sales.

Collectible Canvas Store, Creve Coeur, MO   Summer 1992
Framer
Handled frame/glass cutting and mounting of prints and artwork.

■ Summary of qualifications highlights Joan's acquired skills.
■ College activities are related to Joan's field of study and career objective.

MATHEMATICS MAJOR

Joan Smith

Current Address	**Permanent Address**
178 Green Street	23 Blue Street
Sioux Falls, SD 57103	Wounded Knee, SD 57794
(605) 555-5555	(605) 444-4444

Education: Back Hills State College, Spearfish, SD
Bachelor of Science, May 1994
Concentrations: **Mathematics and Economics**
Independent Study: Comparison of Six Women Mathematicians

Dakota Wesleyan College, Mitchell, SD
September 1990 to May 1992
Concentrations: **Mathematics and Economics**

Memberships:
Debate Club
Economics Faculty/Student Liaison Committee
Mathematics Faculty/Student Liaison Committee

Special Skills: Basic Programming, Fortran Programming, COBOL Programming, Accounting, Word Processing

Experience:

1/94 - Present **Research Analyst**, South Dakota Urban Reinvestment Advisory Group, Sioux Falls, SD. Senior internship. Research and analyze the lending policies of banks.

1/94 - Present **Computer Consultant**, Micro-Computer Laboratory, Estelline, SD Assist students, faculty, and alumni with software and hardware problems.

9/93-12/93 **FORTRAN Tutor**, Black Hills State College, Spearfish, SD

5/93-8/93 **Customer Service Representative**, Oacoma Savings Bank, Oacoma, SD. Handled up to 350 transactions per eight hour day. Processed all address changes for main bank and four branches. Used computers to enter all data.

9/92-5/93 **Mathematics Tutor**, Ecumenical Social Action Committee, Spearfish, SD

Activities:

9/90-5/92 **Big Brother/Big Sister Program**, Mitchell, SD
Participated in a one-to-one relationship with a disadvantaged child.

9/90-5/91 **Political Campaign Worker**, Worked on political campaigns of various candidates for state and national offices.

- Listing a permanent address in addition to a school address is a good idea for students who have not yet graduated.
- Activities section highlights Joan's involvement in her local community.

PSYCHOLOGY MAJOR

Joan Smith
233 Vetnor Avenue
Oklahoma City, OK 93304
(701) 555-5555

Education
1991-
Present

FURMAN UNIVERSITY   **GREENVILLE, SOUTH CAROLINA**
Candidate for the degree of Bachelor of Arts degree in June 1995, majoring in Psychology and minoring in Sociology. Courses included: Public Speaking, Mathematics, and Computer Science. Independent Study topic: The Psychological Impact of Commercial Advertising on Teenage Eating Disorders. Won the Alfred Pinder Award for Outstanding Students of Psychology in 1993.

Teaching Assistant for Introductory Psychology class. Member of Furman Cycling Club. Volunteer for local food shelter. Helped organize on-campus food donation drive for the needy; collected over one-half ton of food that was distributed to over 75 different families.

Summer
1994

OXFORD UNIVERSITY   **OXFORD, ENGLAND**
Participated in summer abroad program, studying English popular culture. Thesis topic: The Role of Music in the English Punk Sub-Culture.

Experience
Summer
1993

THE COCA-COLA COMPANY   **GREENVILLE, SOUTH CAROLINA**
Public Relations Assistant. Wrote promotional material, sent out mass mailings, and in charge of company sponsorship in various charitable events.

Summer
1992

ANNIE'S CANDIES   **GREENVILLE, SOUTH CAROLINA**
Assistant candy-maker and counter person for local sweets shop.

Part-time
1991-1994

Part-time positions include Mail Clerk for college dormitory, Bus-Person at local restaurant, and Pizza Delivery Person.

Interests

Enjoy hiking, cycling, and building model cars. Compete in state-wide cycling races.

References

Personal references available upon request.

- Special academic award, independent study topic, teaching assistant position, and volunteer experience give Joan a competitive edge.
- Part-time employment during college indicates Joan's ability to handle multiple responsibilities.

Joan Smith
178 Green Street
Seattle, WA 98104
(206) 555-5555

OBJECTIVE:
An entry-level position in administration.

SUMMARY:

- Precise and accurate worker with background demonstrating pride in performance and successful work accomplishment.
- Strong problem solving, organizational and communicative skills, paying professional attention to detail.
- Welcome new challenges, quickly learning new skills and procedures with excellent memory retention.

EDUCATION:

RYDELL HIGH SCHOOL, Seattle, WA
Activities: Editor-in-Chief, School Newspaper; Literary Editor, Yearbook; Captain, Drill Team, 1994.

EXPERIENCE:

LANCELOT NATIONAL BANK, Seattle, WA
Customer Service Representative (6/94-Present)
Open new accounts, take applications and process loans, handle customer transactions, cross-sell bank products, purchase supplies, and resolve customer problems and complaints. Other duties include collection of overdrawn accounts, answer telephones, utilize CRT, and clerical duties (light typing, filing).
Winner of Premier Performance Award.

MY SPECIAL PLACE, Seattle, WA
Sales Associate - Children's Department (9/93-6/94)
Provide sales and customer service, resolve customer problems, receive merchandise, arrange displays, set up sales and operational paperwork, i.e., price mark downs, transfers.

- Department Selling Star, among Top Five Salespeople in the store, Fall 1993.
- Award for opening most store credit cards, December 1993.

DAMON AND BLAINE, Seattle, WA (11/92-6/93)
Sales Associate - Linens

WINDSOR SPORTING GOODS, Seattle, WA (1/92-9/92)
Sales Associate - Promoted to Lead Sales Associate.

- Joan's job descriptions indicate how she contributed to her previous employers.
- Extracurricular and work-related awards add weight to Joan's resume.

RECENT GRAD SCHOOL GRAD

Joan Smith
178 Green Street
Plymouth, New Hampshire 03264
(603) 555-5555

EDUCATION

Plymouth State University, Plymouth, NH
M.A. in Marketing, Dec. 1994
Courses include International Marketing, Marketing Research, Business Communications, and Statistics.
Member, National Honor Society.
Pratt University, Brooklyn, NY
B.A. in Accounting, 1992

EMPLOYMENT

THE PLYMOUTH PLAYER, Plymouth, NH

6/94 - Present New Hampshire's largest daily newspaper (circulation 30,000)
Marketing Assistant (part-time)

- Design and manage market research to determine the satisfaction of former subscribers with editorial content. Supplement data with focus group research.
- Develop strategic marketing plans. Propose new marketing management strategies and systems; studied on-line news distribution, and creation of new print publications.
- Initiate telemarketing campaign to sell ads for a special section. Targeted advertisers outside usual geographic territory. Although 1/10 of salesforce, sold 1/3 of total ads (sold 6.0k of total sales of 20k).
- Selling display advertising space. Meet with advertisers, negotiate prices and design ads.

PILGRIM TRAVEL, Plymouth, NH

1/94 - 6/94 Discount travel company specializing in trans-Atlantic cruises
Marketing Intern

- Managed nation wide client base. Monitored sales, marketing, research, analysis, reports and presentations.
- Developed and executed marketing plan. Coordinated marketing communications, published monthly client newsletter, created, marketed and conducted seminars, and managed direct mail campaigns.
- Analyzed finances of client organizations. Performed analysis of multivariate revenue, insurance revenue, and accounts receivable.

COMPUTERS

IBM: WordPerfect, Lotus 1-2-3; Macintosh: Microsoft Word.

REFERENCES

Available upon request.

- Part-time work experience during school indicates Joan's strong work ethic.
- Stating that "references are available upon request" is not essential; most employers will assume that references are available.

ACCOUNTANT

JOAN SMITH
178 Green Street
Billings, MT 59105
(406) 555-5555

EMPLOYMENT HISTORY

July 1989 to Present **ROSS PECOE, INC., Billings, MT**
(A $20 million publicly held company that develops, manufactures, and markets proprietary x-ray systems)
Senior Financial Analyst/Accountant (July, 1990 to Present)
- Assist controller in preparation of financial statements and all SEC reporting.
- Assist in the consolidation of three European subsidiaries.
- Review work of staff accountant and approve journal transactions for data entry.
- Assist with the corporate budget in preparation and maintenance of budgets and projections using both Excel and Lotus for Windows.
- Prepare monthly budget to actual reports and distribute to managers.
- Manage accounting duties of a venture capital funded start-up organization, Beta Technologies, Inc. (sister company to Ross Pecoe Inc.), including financial reporting and coordinating annual audit with external auditors.
- Implemented the ASK ManMan computer information system.

Senior Accountant (July, 1989 to July, 1990)
- Assisted with monthly closings and financial reporting.
- Worked directly with controller in preparation for Primary and Secondary Public Stock Offerings.
- Implemented Solomon III General Ledger Accounting Package, including the installation and set-up of all modules required by accounting, the development of procedures to be used by this new system, the training of staff on the system, and the formatting of several financial reports.
- Installed and maintained a seven-user Novell Network.

March 1987 to July 1989 **STEADFAST CORP., Cherry Creek, MT**
(A venture capital-funded software development firm)
Staff Accountant
- Administered single-user Solomon III Accounting System.
- Assisted in general ledger close including foreign currency translation of foreign subsidiaries.
- Monitored cash and accounts receivable.
- Trained new employees to administer the accounts payable and order entry functions.

EDUCATION

Bronte College, New Castle, ME
Master of Science in Accountancy, expected completion August, 1993
Carroll College, Helena, MT
Bachelor of Arts in Business Management, December, 1986

COMPUTER SKILLS

Excel, Lotus 1-2-3 (Windows), ASK ManMan General Ledger, Solomon General Ledger, Novell Network

- Joan's computer skills are highlighted in a separate section.
- Brief descriptions of employers add weight to Joan's already strong qualifications.

ACCOUNT MANAGER

JOAN SMITH
178 Green Street
Winchester, VA 22001
(703) 555-5555

Experience:

	Starbuck Computer, Inc.	Richmond, VA

10/93 to **National Account Manager**
present Responsibilities include developing and implementing national sales strategy for several Richmond-based *Fortune* 500 corporations including Ackler Industrial, The Carnulton Group, Hanlon and Associates, and Polamin Company. Position requires the identification and analysis of potential business applications within target accounts and the cultivation of key business relationships with senior management to facilitate sales.

- Average performance over five year period was 125%
- Grew Starbuck revenue 200% to $5M amidst decreasing unit pricing and increasing sales goals
- Completed all five years in the top 12% of the National Account Channel and received Golden Star Award every year
- Created new revenue streams resulting in an estimated $300M in Starbuck sales and $400M in new services for the company

10/85 to **Dealer Account Executive**
10/93 Responsible for the sale of Starbuck products into dealer locations. Initiated cooperative sales strategy with reseller business owners, designed marketing promotions, and directed reseller's sales efforts into business and education accounts.

- Average performance over six year period was 110%
- Grew sales by 400% to $11M
- Received Golden Star Club Award every year

7/80 to **Corporate Chain Account Sales Representative**
10/85 Provided administrative and technical sales support to Richmond corporate chain account locations including Power Electronics, Computer Corral and Circonne Computer. Developed marketing promotions and trained store personnel.

10/77 to **Customer Support Representative**
7/80 Created and implemented customer service procedures for Richmond distribution facility. Resolved customer service issues including invoicing discrepancies, shipping errors and upgrades for hardware.

Education:
5/77 Randolph-Macon College   Lynchburg, VA
B.A., Communications and Political Science

- Specific dates of employment (month and year) are ideal for candidates with no gaps in work history.
- Education is de-emphasized because Joan's work history is strong.

ACCOUNTS RECEIVABLE CLERK

JOAN SMITH

---

178 Green Street   Newark, NJ 07107   (201) 555-5555

CAREER HISTORY

THE FULLER COMPANY, Newark, NJ   1990-Present
Assistant Manager—Accounts Receivable
- Maintained $10,000 petty cash fund and $15,000 American Express Travelers' Checks account.
- Documented "proofed" checks and moneys for deposit and coordinated with other departments to resolve problems with checks that failed to clear.
- Posted receivables to electronic spreadsheet (Lotus 1-2-3) and month-end journal entries on MILLENNIUM system—a highly technical software application.
- Researched interdepartmental queries and provided results to requester.
- Performed traditional accounting functions.

Financial Associate-Accounts Payable
- Audited documents to include expense reports, invoices, and check requests for payment.
- Generated disbursement instructions for accounts.
- Assigned and maintained vendor identification files through an on-line computer system.
- Developed and maintained 1099 tax information on vendor.
- Assisted in establishing and validating travel reimbursement programs.

B. PARR AND ASSOCIATES, West Orange, NJ   1988-1990
Bookkeeper
- Performed all accounting functions to include journal entries, accounts payables, receivables, petty cash, deposits, bank reconciliations, and trial balance.
- Calculated payroll deductions and processed payroll.
- Responsible for monthly, quarterly and year end payroll and sales tax forms.
- Effective in phone collection of overdue accounts, generating invoices and statements.

HACKENSACK HOME FURNISHINGS, Hackensack, NJ   1985-1988
Manager/Bookkeeper
- Brought company to full operational status.
- Responsible for inventory, orders, sales, rent-to-own contracts
- Supervisor of part-time employees.
- Performed all bookkeeping, banking, sales, payroll taxes, and bank reconciliations.

EDUCATION

Kean College of New Jersey, Union, N.J.
AS in Accounting, December 1984.

- Use of concrete examples accentuates Joan's achievements.
- Chronological format illustrates a clear career path.

ADMINISTRATIVE ASSISTANT

JOAN SMITH
178 Green Street
Dallas, TX 75275
(214) 555-5555

OBJECTIVE

To secure a challenging position as an Administrative Assistant.

SUPPORTIVE QUALIFICATIONS

- 3 years as an administrative assistant.
- 4 years experience working in the medical/health care arena.
- 2 years education and training in Secretarial Sciences.

STRENGTHS

Detail-oriented	Organized
Patient	Prioritize Accurately
Positive Attitude	Work Well Under Pressure

PROFESSIONAL EXPERIENCE

MUSTANG DISTRIBUTORS, Dallas, TX   **Administrative Assistant**
1993-Present Performed general secretarial tasks, typing reports, and correspondence on Macintosh equipment; arranged meetings, expense reports, and travel vouchers. Designed computer automation system; assisted in its implementation.

TEXAS MEDICAL CENTER, Austin, TX   **Unit Secretary**
1990-Present Transcribed doctors' orders for patients' records on computer; answered telephones in busy office.

GRANITE INVESTMENT RESOURCE CENTER, Dallas, TX   **Data Entry**
1988-1990 Input account transactions and transfers into computer.

SEUSS HEALTH, Houston, TX   **Data Entry**
1986-1988 Input medical information, maintained computer files; managed nightly upkeep and documentation of triage information, medication, and treatments.

BROWNWOOD HOSPITAL, El Paso, TX**File Clerk, Medical Records Department**
1984-1986 Filed, answered phones, researched patient information for various departments.

EDUCATION

DALLAS COMMUNITY COLLEGE; course work in Secretarial Sciences and Business, 1984-1986.

REFERENCES

Furnished upon request.

- Layout is clean and well-organized.
- Joan's resume includes course work that corresponds to the position desired.

ADVERTISING COORDINATOR

JOAN SMITH
178 Green Street
Hammond, VA 70402
(504) 555-5555

OBJECTIVE

A challenging career in the advertising industry.

SUMMARY OF QUALIFICATIONS

- Eight years of progressive professional administrative, advertising, and client service experience.
- Self-motivated; able to set effective priorities and implement decisions to achieve immediate and long-term goals and meet operational deadlines.
- Adapt easily to new concepts and responsibilities.

PROFESSIONAL EXPERIENCE

BRADFORD'S DEPARTMENT STORE, Hammond, VA

Advertising Coordinator   1991-Present

Coordinate weekly, monthly, and seasonal advertising and sales campaigns. Actuate/update weekly advertising planning calendars. Input into computer system. Generate confidential reports and monthly communication packages; interact with Production Department and store managers. Update ad changes. Maintain/update media contracts and ratebook. Recreated daily calendar history for 92/93 season; verified information accuracy; entered into word processor.

Print Media Coordinator - Remote Stores   1990-1991

Planned, updated, and managed monthly remote market information; issued forecasts. Acted as liaison with Media Representatives, Store Executives, and Production Department in planning and problem solving. Developed strategies and budget recommendations. Required extensive knowledge of remote markets, media availability and coverage, and rate structures.

Advertising Administrator   1988-1990

Coordinated confidential reports and communication packages for seasonal planbook. Maintained media files. Gathered/entered historical data into weekly and monthly planbook. Dealt with storewide and direct mail information requiring strict adherence to deadlines. Coordinated/oversaw development of newspaper ad system.

XRAY VISION, Winchester, VA   1986-1988

Sales Representative/Telemarketer

Supervised/scheduled personnel. Headed payroll administration 100-member staff.

EDUCATION

UNIVERSITY OF VIRGINIA, Charlottesville, VA

B.A., Communications   1986

- Summary of qualifications is concise and adds punch to resume.
- For upward-bound professionals with a strong track record, the chrono-functional resume is the strongest tool available.

APPLICATIONS PROGRAMMER

JOAN SMITH
178 Green Street
New York, NY 10003
(718) 555-5555

EMPLOYMENT
HISTORY

BENTLEY LIFE INSURANCE, New York, NY   1988-Present
Programmer Analyst/Senior Programmer

- Supervised and guided junior programmers in the team on various PC Illustration System Projects.
- Developed, maintained, and supported Sales Illustration Systems in "C."
- Developed a Front End System for the Bentley Sales Illustration Systems in OS/2 Presentation Manager.
- Wrote the "Illustration Software Installation" routine in INSTALIT software.
- Designed a file transfer process to and from the Mainframe to PC using NDM (Network Data Mover) software.
- Hands-on experience with PC hardware, DOS, MS Windows, IBM OS/2, Novell Software, Emulation Software (Rumba, Extra, etc.), Dial-In Software (SimPC, XTalk, etc.) and have understanding of Token Ring LAN.
- Wrote DOS Batch files for Illustration Software Installation routine.
- Developed an Executive Information System on the mainframe using COBOL 2. Became very familiar with mainframe production environment.
- Maintained and supported the existing COBOL mainframe on-line and batch systems.

SHADOW ASSOCIATES, Hartford, CT   1986-1988
Computer Programmer

- Designed product and sales tracking programs for company computer system.
- Monitored product availability and inventory for branch sites, display new product releases and access daily proceed information.
- Maintained/expanded client base.

EDUCATION

New York University, New York, NY
Master of Science in Electrical Engineering, 1986
Program emphasis: Software Engineering and Computer Networks

Oxford University, Oxford, England
Bachelor of Science in Engineering (Electronics Option), 1984
Program emphasis: Digital Communications and Engineering Management

TECHNICAL
SUMMARY

Hardware:	IBM PC, IBM Mainframe
Software:	MS Windows, Rumba, Novell
Op Systems:	MS-DOS, OS-2, MVS
Languages:	C, COBOL, COBOL II, Pascal, FORTRAN, Visual Basic, Assembly

- Joan's job descriptions include technical jargon specific to her field.
- Bullets make resume easy to read.

ARCHITECT

JOAN SMITH
178 Green Street
East Brunswick, NJ 08816
(908) 555-5555

SUMMARY
Over seven years in Architecture and Facility Management (FM) related industries with emphasis in Computer Design Base (CDB), Education, and Communication.

PROFESSIONAL EXPERIENCE
CDB INC., East Brunswick, NJ   1992-Present
Architect
Provide industry consultation and implementation expertise in architecture and FM, Computer-Aided Design and Database Management software packages. Experience with IBM Mainframe, Workstation, and PC based products.
- Provide demonstration, presentations and technical support for pre- and post-sales activity
- Act as subject matter expert for future software enhancements and requirements
- Lead role in various joint studies teaming with IBM and other major corporations in the evaluation CDB software for architecture

CITY OF PITTSBURGH, Pittsburgh, PA   1988-1992
Building Inspector
Worked within both the Public and Private Sector. Required knowledge of local government agency procedures (e.g. obtaining permits, variances, interfacing with the Building, Planning, and Engineering Departments). Projects included:
- Commercial and industrial interior spaces
- Small commercial and low-rise buildings
- Large customer and multi-family residential housing
- Architectural renderings, presentation graphics

PROFESSIONAL REGISTRATIONS
LICENSED ARCHITECT - State of New Jersey   C100468

EDUCATION
MASTER OF ARCHITECTURE   1988
University of Pennsylvania
Philadelphia, PA

BACHELOR OF SCIENCE, ARCHITECTURE 1986
Massachusetts Institute of Technology
Cambridge, MA

COMPUTER SKILLS
DOS, IBM, Microsoft Word, Pascal, Lotus 1-2-3

- Summary highlights Joan's experience and expertise in her field.
- Including professional licensure and accreditations can be essential for certain fields of work.

ASSOCIATE EDITOR

Joan Smith
178 Green Street
Little Rock, AR 72204
(501) 555-5555

WORK EXPERIENCE

Senior Editor   May 1994-Present
THE SOUTHWEST TRAVEL REPORT   Little Rock, AR
Develop and manage editorial direction and content of start-up monthly regional
trade journal covering travel industry. Instrumental in content development and
design. Assign and manage contributing writers, report, and wrote stories for
publication prototype, coordinate art and production elements.

Associate Editor   April 1992-May 1994
THE JENSEN COMPANY   Little Rock, AR
Reported and wrote features for five departments for three trade magazines
covering the meeting, convention, and incentive travel industries. Assisted in the
development of story and art ideas as well as copyediting and proofing.

Assistant Editor   Dec. 1991-March 1992
DEYLAH PUBLISHING   Little Rock, AR
Researched and wrote items for annual fact books and their weekly supplemental
updates covering communications industry.

Contributing Editor   Sept. 1988-Nov. 1991
WHERE TO EAT   Little Rock, AR
Wrote articles for monthly restaurant trade newspaper.

Administrative Assistant   April-June 1988
CONWAY ARTS JOURNAL   Conway, AR
Assisted business and marketing directors in direct mail projects, classified
advertising, and fulfillment of book and subscription orders.

Editorial Intern   Sept.-Dec. 1987
CONWAY ARTS JOURNAL   Conway, AR
Reported and wrote articles and columns for twice monthly newspaper for the arts
and entertainment industry. Position also involved research, fact checking, and
production support.

EDUCATION

Hendrix College, Conway, AR
B.A. degree, English/Political Science, 1988
Member-The Society of Professional Journalists

- Joan's resume indicates a series of promotions.
- Joan lists her education towards the bottom of her resume because her practical experience outweighs her degree.

ATTORNEY

JOAN SMITH
178 Green Street
Bangor, ME 04401
(207) 555-5555

Admitted to Maine Bar, 1987
Admitted to Indiana Bar, 1986

EDUCATION
INDIANA UNIVERSITY, Bloomington, IN
Master of Studies in Environmental Law and Public Policy, magna cum laude, 1987
Juris Doctor, 1986
Environmental Action Group; National Lawyers Guild Indiana Chapter

ROCKFORD COLLEGE, Rockford, IL
Bachelor of Arts, 1983 Major: Sociology, cum laude
Editor, Environmental Newsletter

PROFESSIONAL EXPERIENCE
MAINE ENVIRONMENTAL RESEARCH GROUP, Waterville, ME   July 1988-Present
Environmental Program Director/Attorney
Coordinate environmental programs; develop policies; oversee campaign activities and staff. Draft legislation. Provide legal counseling. Develop media relations. Serve on state's acid rain and recycling program advisory committees. Initiated and successfully lobbied for state-wide moratorium on mandatory recycling. Strengthened state's acid rain regulations.

SOLO PRACTICE   August 1986-June 1988
Practiced before Water Resources Board. Negotiated small claims settlements; conducted title searches; advised clients on permitting processes.

LEGISLATIVE COUNCIL, 1985 Indiana General Assembly, Indianapolis, IN   Spring, 1985
Intern
Conducted legal research. Wrote memoranda. Presented testimony and drafted legislation primarily for House and Senate Health and Welfare and Government Operations committees. Worked with legislators, public and private interests. Addressed issues including toxics regulation, employment discrimination, and health care financing.

LAND USE CLINIC, Indiana University, Bloomington, IN   Fall, 1985
Investigated/analyzed Indiana design review ordinances. Searched records; attended administrative proceedings; interviewed planning officials; submitted report with recommendations for improving existing state enabling statute.

INDIANA ENVIRONMENTAL CONSERVATION BUREAU, Indianapolis, IN   Fall, 1984
Semester in Practice, Dept. of Hazardous Waste
Served on legislatively mandated advisory committee. Acted as liaison to Attorney General's office on uncontrolled hazardous waste cases. Addressed issues including pollution liability insurance, water protection, and non-hazardous waste disposal.

- Resume provides Joan's most essential qualification, bar accreditation, at the top of the page.
- Dynamic action verbs give Joan's resume impact.

BANK TELLER

```
                         JOAN SMITH
                      178 Green Street
                     Baltimore, MD 21202
                       (301) 555-5555
```

OBJECTIVE
To utilize banking and sales experience, in the Hospitality or
Business arena.

SUMMARY OF QUALIFICATIONS

- Skilled in the production and dissemination of correspondence, materials management, maintenance of filing systems, mail processing, and data entry.
- Proficient in the execution of banking processes, daily transaction reconciliation, sale of bank products, customer service, consistent input of recommendations for procedural enhancement, and personnel management.

PROFESSIONAL EXPERIENCE

1989 -
Present **BANK OF BALTIMORE, Teller**   Baltimore, MD

- Process various account transactions, reconcile and deposit daily funds.
- Inform customers of bank products, refer public to designated personnel, provide account status data, and handle busy phone.
- Execute signature functions and provide input for system enhancement.
- Orient, train, supervise, and delegate tasks for new hires.
- Serve as Team Leader for Christmas Clothing Campaign for Homeless.

1987-98 **MEYER, GREEN AND FAZIO, Office Assistant**   Princess Anne, MD

- Collected, sorted, and distributed incoming mail. Processed outgoing mail.

1986-87 **TANNENBAUM SOCIETY, Sales Associate**   Washington, DC

- Serviced customers, reconciled cash drawer.
- Created effective product displays.

1984-86 **KENT AND LANE ASSOCIATES, Office Assistant**   Richmond, VA

- Produced correspondence, responded to public inquiries, monitored and maintained confidential records.

EDUCATION

GENEVA COLLEGE, Annapolis, MD
Associate degree in Business/Travel, 1984

COMPUTERS

Lotus 1-2-3, WordPerfect 5.1, IBM Compatible, Sabre

- Typewritten resumes are generally acceptable for administrative and office support positions.
- Company names and dates are listed on the left margin while locations are listed on the right margin.

CHEMIST

JOAN SMITH
178 Green Street
Norfolk, MA 02056
(508) 555-5555

PROFESSIONAL OBJECTIVE
A responsible and challenging position in the field of chemistry.

PROFESSIONAL BACKGROUND

1983 to
Present
BOSTON HOSPITAL, Boston, MA
Chemist
- Responsible for conducting more than 500 manual and computerized assays of steroids, carcinogenic analyses, vitamins, fibrinogens, and other chemicals in hospital laboratory.
- Position involves rotation of duties and includes usage of the following instrumentation: HPLC, GSC, Nephelometer, Boehringer-Mannheim Multichannel Analyzer, Beckman Astra, Centrifichem, Spectrofluoromter, Electrophoresis, Spectrophotometer, and Flame Photometry.
- Knowledge of quality control systems and techniques.
- Perform maintenance and ensure proper calibration of instrumentation.
- Interface with physicians regarding test results and methodology.
- Train new employees.

1980 to
1981
TUFTS UNIVERSITY CHEMISTRY DEPARTMENT, Medford, MA
Teaching Assistant
- Instructed General Chemistry classes and laboratories.

1979
MASSACHUSETTS INSTITUTE OF TECHNOLOGY, Cambridge, MA
Guest Speaker
- Planned and conducted 3-day seminar on analysis of metals in soil for national chemistry convention.

EDUCATIONAL BACKGROUND
FLORIDA INSTITUTE OF TECHNOLOGY, Melbourne, FL
Master's Degree Program in Chemistry (1980-1985)

FLORIDA INTERNATIONAL UNIVERSITY
Bachelor of Science Degree with Honors in Chemistry (1979)
- Thesis: Analysis of Metals in Soil

CERTIFICATION
Certified in Chemistry by ASCP

- Bullets make Joan's resume easy to read.
- Professional certification adds weight to Joan's credentials.

CIVIL ENGINEER

JOAN SMITH
178 Green Street
Bryn Mawr, PA 19010
(215) 555-5555

EMPLOYMENT HIGHLIGHTS

1987-Present Kershaw and Kane Inc., Bryn Mawr, PA
Specialist in the Structural Division
Prepare technical guidelines and master specifications, review project specifications, maintain technical files and bidder lists, provide technical expertise in areas relating to fire resistance, combustibility of building materials and systems in general. Act as a liaison between design and manufacturing in introductions of notebook and desktop products. Create initial process methods, documentation, line balancing, tooling, and fixturing for new and existing products.

1984-87 Bradford A. Sullivan Corp., Meadville, PA
Assistant Manager of the Construction Section
Served as backup to and acted in the absence of the manager. Prepared technical guides for property conservation in the areas of wind, fire, gravity loads, and earthquakes. Performed loss investigations and special inspections in areas of interest. As a staff lecturer, conducted training classes and seminars. Reviewed plans and specifications for loss potential.

1981-84 Dixon & Petrie Division, Pittsburgh, PA
Structural Designer.
Provided structural design and engineering estimates, and specifications for industrial, laboratory, commercial, and power facilities.

1977-81 Building Blocks, Inc., Boston, MA
Structural Designer.
Provided structural design and engineering estimates for highway bridges and waterworks.

1974-77 Stephen G. Fox, Inc., Artemis, PA
Engineer
Participated in bid and cost-plus work, structural design, engineering field supervision, engineering estimates, construction (bid) estimates, and construction coordination on industrial and commercial projects.

LICENSURE Professional Engineer - Pennsylvania

EDUCATION New York University, New York, NY
Bachelor of Science, Civil Engineering, 1973

- Resume illustrates Joan's continual career progression.
- Including professional licensure and accreditations can be essential for certain fields of work.

CUSTOMER SERVICE REPRESENTATIVE

JOAN SMITH
178 Green Street
Broken Arrow, OK 74011
(918) 555-5555

SUMMARY OF QUALIFICATIONS

- Demonstrated ability in the provision of sales support services. Includes establishment of the client base, extensive customer servicing, telemarketing, cold calling, and sales territory development.
- Consistently met/exceeded sales goals and instituted sales programs; sales increased from $8 to $25 million.
- Thorough knowledge of management production; assure timely and accurate presentation of goods; adept at coordinating delivery processes, organization of delivery schedules, and monitoring delivery personnel.
- Extensive experience in facilitating operational procedures. Respond to customer complaints; resolve problem elements; interact with credit department to ascertain customer account status. Handle sourcing of vendors, contract negotiation, purchasing, correspondence, account adjustments, and inventory control.
- Exceptional communication/interpersonal and organizational skills.

EXPERIENCE

OXBRIDGE, INC.   Broken Arrow, OK
Sales/Customer Service Representative   **1989-Present**

- Interface with merchandising personnel at all levels, and provide technical information on company products and services.
- Interact with customers, providing advice in the selection of products. Monitor production to ensure realization of customer specifications.
- Collaborate with contracting merchandisers for contract negotiation on supplies. Conduct extensive materials costing processes.
- Coordinate delivery schedules and monitor delivery personnel.
- Organize promotional demonstration activities for home and New York marketing office.
- Respond to and resolve customer complaints.
- Manage office operations and produce correspondence.
- Control stock and conduct purchasing procedures.
- Assist sales department in establishing client base/sales territories.

EDUCATION

PROPHET JUNIOR COLLEGE   Broken Arrow, OK
Associate Degree Program   **1993 to Present**
Computer Operations Program: Lotus 1-2-3, Database III, Typing, Word processing (Multimate), Business Math, Speech Communication, Introduction to Computers, and English Composition.

- Background summary accentuates Joan's acquired professional skills and impressive track record.
- Listing relevant courses adds weight to Joan's educational credentials.

DENTAL HYGIENIST

JOAN SMITH
178 Green Street
Upper Montclair, NJ
(201) 555-5555

OBJECTIVE
A full-time position as a Dental Hygienist in a private practice.

EMPLOYMENT
Dr. Rettman, D.M.D., Upper Montclair, NJ
Dental Hygienist   (1988 to present)
- Provide prophylaxis treatment to patients in a variety of situations; teeth cleaning, gum massage, oral hygiene education, and periodontal scaling.
- Monitor radiographs. Administer novocaine prior to painful procedures.
- Provide secretarial assistance: telephones, paperwork, scheduling, etc.

Dr. Grohowski, D.M.D., Princeton, NJ
Dental Assistant   (1985 to 1988)
- Assisted dentist in prophylactic procedures: provided necessary tools, sterilized equipment, comforted patients.

EDUCATION
Kelly School of Dental Hygiene, New York, NY
A.S. in Dental Hygiene, 1985
Course work included: Chemistry, Radiology, Nutrition, Periodontology, Pathology, Anatomy, Dental Equipment, Oral Embiology, Psychology, and Pharmacology.

LICENSURE
New Jersey Dental Hygiene License
National Board Dental Hygiene Exam (written - 90)
N.E.R.B. Dental Hygiene Exam (Clinical - 93, written -90)

REFERENCES
Available upon request.

- Joan's job objective is brief and to the point.
- Use of boldface and italics provides a clean and crisp presentation.

DESKTOP PUBLISHER

JOAN SMITH
178 Green Street
Revere, MA 02151
(617)555-5555

PROFILE

Experienced design professional with background in desktop publishing, graphic design, and technical art. Proficient in Ventura Publisher 4.0, PerForm Form Designer, Micrografx Designer, QuarkXpress and WordPerfect 5.1.

EXPERIENCE

LYERLA LIFE INSURANCE COMPANY, Revere, MA   1992-Present
DESKTOP PUBLISHER

- Produced brochures, personnel forms, and policy pages using WordPerfect 5.1, PerForm, Ventura, Designer and quark in a Windows environment.
- Created layout and design of brochures detailing product lines for sales representatives and convention participants. Worked with sales representatives and printers regarding bid specifications and deadlines for three color brochures.
- Extensive experience in WordPerfect designing and formatting over 350 policy pages.

KANE INC., Welch, WV   1988-1992
TECHNICAL ILLUSTRATOR/GRAPHIC DESIGNER

- Created complex diagrams, schedules, charts, and signs for use in proposals, reports, and division communications. Designed and updated organization charts for division.
- Designed and formatted an eight-page employee newsletter. Sized photos and used stat camera for art. Worked with outside vendors for photos and final printing of newsletter.
- Produced photo contest poster, Employee of the Year poster, booklets, brochures, and invitations promoting company events.
- Within TQM environment assumed management responsibility, prioritized assignments, delegated tasks and planned schedules. Prepared material for presentation by TQM groups.
- Organized and led departmental meetings, successfully resolving problems with product quality. Established department standards for artwork and documents; published handbook of standards implemented department wide.

JUNIOR TECHNICAL ILLUSTRATOR/TECHNICAL TYPIST   1982-1988

- Responsible for technical drawings, newspaper paste-up, diagrams, and illustrations for technical reports and proposals. Assisted photographer in photo lab.
- Typeset copy for proposals and viewgraph presentations using Wang word processor and IBM Composer. Typing speed 80+wpm.

EDUCATION

University of Tennessee, Knoxville, TN
Graphic Design Certificate, 1982

Benkart Junior College, Benkart, TN
WordPerfect 5.1 Applications, 1981

- Profile grabs the reader's attention with powerful skills and qualifications.
- Joan's resume emphasizes her achievements, rather than simply listing her job responsibilities.

DIRECTOR OF HUMAN RESOURCES

JOAN SMITH
178 Green Street
Memphis, TN 38116
(901) 555-5555

OBJECTIVE
A career in Personnel Management/Administration.

PROFESSIONAL EXPERIENCE

TENNESSEE PAROLE BOARD   Memphis, TN
Director of Human Resources and Staff Development   1991-Present
Develop and implement policy. Provide leadership in the areas of personnel, payroll, labor relations, training, and affirmative action. Administer personnel/payroll system to meet management and employee needs. Consult with Chairman, Executive Director, managerial staff, and supervisors to ensure policy compliance with applicable statutes, rules, and regulations. Advance agency Affirmative Action Plan. Determine appropriate grievance procedures relief; resolve labor disputes. Act as liaison for regulatory agencies: EOHS, OER, DPA, State Office of A.A., and PERA. Maintain staff training program. Interface with Legal Staff in dealing with progressive discipline and grievances.

WILMONT INSURANCE CO.   Nashville, TN
Director of Human Resources   1987-1991
Maintained smooth workflow; supervised claim adjudication; performed claim payment internal audits; coordinated activity with reinsurance carriers. Hired/terminated, trained, oversaw, and delegated personnel. Determined technical decisions and payments. Responsible for computer maintenance (IBM Series I) and updating personnel files to ensure compliance with state/local regulations pertaining to holidays, vacations, etc.

Central Personnel Officer   1984-1987
Coordinated statewide reclassification study; organized questionnaires, individual interviews and desk audits. Evaluated/analyzed study data; rewrote job descriptions; prepared study package for legislative approval. Established related managerial files. Dealt with diverse personnel-related projects.

EDUCATION
Milligan College   Milligan College, TN
Course work in Personnel Management and Human Resources 1990-Present

Tennessee Wesleyan College   Nashville, TN
B.A. Degree, Management   1980

- Reverse chronological format focuses employer's attention on Joan's most current position.
- Continuing education indicates Joan's ongoing commitment to her career.

DISTRICT MANAGER

JOAN SMITH
178 Green Street
Chickasha, OK 73023
(405) 555-5555

OBJECTIVE:

A district management position. Willing to travel and/or relocate.

PROFESSIONAL EXPERIENCE:

JESSAMINE BOOKSTORES INC., Chickasha, OK
District Manager, Oklahoma   1991-Present

- Oversee all operations of ten retail bookstores in Oklahoma.
- Advise store management on personnel functions, merchandising, loss prevention, and customer service; communicate and ensure compliance with company policies, procedures, and programs.
- Open new stores; hire staff; oversee initial set-up.
- Research competition relative to title selection, pricing, merchandising, and sales programs.

WHIPPORWHILLBOOKS, New York, NY
District Manager, West Coast   1988-91

- Managed operations as above for total of five districts in Los Angeles, San Francisco, San Diego, San Gabriel, and San Fernando.
- Performed extensive hiring, training, and developing of store managers.
- Set individual store and district sales goals.
- Named District Manager of the Year for Western United States, 1990, 1991.

Store Manager, New York   1986-88

- Oversaw daily store operations; hired, trained, and developed personnel; performed merchandising functions; tracked and reported sales; handled inventory, bookkeeping, cash administration, etc.

Assistant Manager, New York   1985-1986

- Assisted manager in day-to-day operations; managed store in his absence.

EDUCATION:

Southwestern University, Georgetown, TX
Bachelor of Arts in English Literature, May 1984

COMPUTERS:

Macintosh FileMaker, Microsoft Word, Spreadsheet, ManagePro

- Indicating a willingness to relocate on a resume can be advantageous.
- Resume indicates a series of promotions.

EMERGENCY MEDICAL TECHNICIAN

Joan Smith
178 Green Street
Visalia, CA 93291
(209) 555-5555

QUALIFICATIONS

- Work well under pressure in crisis situations.
- Thorough knowledge of all Emergency Medical procedures.
- Certified, C.P.R. and Heimlich Methods of Resuscitation.
- Proven capabilities in adhering to standard methods of assisting in emergency childbirth and heart attacks.
- Demonstrated skills in applications of dressings, including burn dressings, tourniquets, oxygen, IVs.
- Familiar with procedures for critical burns, shock, gunshot wounds, physical manifestations of child abuse, and wife battering.
- Provide emergency treatment for rape victims while staying within the guidelines of the law.
- Excellent knowledge of all main streets and secondary routes; strong sense of direction and map reading ability.

LICENSES/CERTIFICATIONS/TRAINING

Certified, E.M.T. License	**Visalia Hospital, 1990**
License #4490223	**State of California, 1990**
Recertification Credits	**California General Hospital, 1994**

E.M.T. EXPERIENCE

DOLAN AMBULANCE SERVICES	**Visalia, CA**
Head Emergency Medical Technician	**1993-Present**

Provide emergency response and care to primarily elderly patients with bone fractures, strokes, heart attacks, falls. Assist in standard hospital and legal procedures for fatalities and post-mortem crises management.

RUSSELL AMBULANCE SERVICES	**Los Angeles, CA**
Emergency Medical Technician	**1990-1993**

Assist in providing emergency response to 911 calls; emergency care to patients involved in traffic accidents, heart attacks, stroke, falls, industrial accidents.

- Qualifications section accentuates Joan's acquired professional skills.
- Joan's necessary licenses/certifications/training are boldfaced for impact.

GRAPHIC ARTIST/DESIGNER

Joan Smith
178 Green Street
Elk Rapids, MI 49629
(517) 555-5555

CAREER OBJECTIVE

A challenging position in the field of COMMERCIAL ART where I can contribute highly developed graphic design skills and technical aptitude.

RELATED EXPERIENCE

GRAPHIC ARTIST   1984-Present
Packard Army Reserves, Elk Rapids, MI
Serve as artistic support for Army Base; create flyers, charts, brochures, tickets, diagrams, maps, and design logos. Document work order requests; plan and organize work to meet all deadline requirements. Purchase materials and supplies; document materials received, and perform graphics department inventory. Maintain accurate and timely department records.

GRAPHIC ARTIST/ELECTRONIC DESIGN   1988-Present
Midland Products, Alden, MI
Produce camera-ready art utilizing Apple computer system with laser printing equipment. Proficient in use of MacDraw, Pagemaker and Freehand programs. Process film, operate reproduction camera for stats, positive and negative images. Utilize Diffusion Transfer machine. Effectively organize time and work to consistently meet critical deadlines. Keep artwork and files up-to-date.

TECHNICAL LINE ARTIST   1984-1988
Marmoset Electric Company, Rapid City, MI
Performed drafting work; inked illustrations. Produced paste-up and mechanical preparation for Detroit Transit Railcar Inspection Manuals.

ARTIST/PASTE UP   1982-1984
Sharona's Art Emporium, Ellsworth, MI
Created art for viewgraphs and slide presentations; designed ads for newspaper; provided computer art for Sharona's computer facility. Set up mechanicals for print orders including business cards and stationery. Ran blueprints, made negatives, and opaqued negatives.

EDUCATION
ASSOCIATE'S DEGREE in GRAPHIC DESIGN, 1980
Kendall School of Design, Grand Rapids, MI

PORTFOLIO AND REFERENCES AVAILABLE UPON REQUEST

- Job objective focuses on the needs of the employer, not the job candidate.
- Stating that a portfolio is available upon request is beneficial for certain positions.

INTERIOR DESIGNER

Joan Smith
178 Green Street
Murfreesboro, TN 37129
(615) 555-5555

PROFESSIONAL OBJECTIVE
A responsible and challenging position as a SENIOR INTERIOR DESIGNER.

SUMMARY OF QUALIFICATIONS
- Broad-based knowledge from over four years of professional experience in architectural and interior design including space planning, product knowledge, specification, and drafting techniques.
- Training and coordination of administrative and operational support personnel, with the ability to work productively and effectively with all levels of management and a full range of personalities.
- Ability to meet deadlines and work well under pressure.
- Exceptional interpersonal, client service, and liaison skills.
- Presentation of a positive and professional image.

EMPLOYMENT HISTORY
1988 to   MERRIMONT BUSINESS SETTINGS, INC., Jackson, TN
Present   <u>Senior Interior Designer</u>
- Responsible with team of six designers for producing space plans and interior finishes for corporate offices, schools, libraries, and banks.
- Developed expertise in field measuring, architectural planning, inventory, product specification, finish selection, renderings and presentation boards, and supervision of installation.
- Enjoy extensive client contact throughout design process including resolution of problems.
- Train and supervise junior designers.
- Plan budgets, make estimates, and negotiate final sales agreement with client.

1985 to   LAWRENCE LOWFERN ASSOCIATES, Nashville, TN
1988   <u>Junior Interior Designer</u>
- Conducted preliminary inventory work, site measurement, drafting of space plans, 1/4 scale details, elevations, choosing and paste-up of finishes on presentation boards, budgets, specification writing, and follow-up work.

EDUCATIONAL BACKGROUND
MEMPHIS COLLEGE OF ART, Memphis, TN
Bachelor of Fine Arts in Interior Design, 1984

Portfolio available upon request

- Chrono-functional resume has the strength of chronological format and the flexibility of functional format.
- Joan's job descriptions are brief and punchy, without being choppy.

LABORATORY ASSISTANT

JOAN SMITH
178 Green Street
Manchester, NH 03102
(603) 555-5555

PROFESSIONAL OBJECTIVE
A challenging and rewarding position as a Laboratory Assistant in the field of Molecular Biology.

EDUCATION
NOTRE DAME COLLEGE, Manchester, New Hampshire
Master of Science degree in Microbiology, 1993

ST. ANSELM COLLEGE, Manchester, New Hampshire
Bachelor of Science degree in Biology, 1991
- Dean's List
- Natural Sciences Department Award
- Senior Class President
- Named to Who's Who in American Colleges and Universities

EXPERIENCE
ST. ANSELM COLLEGE, Manchester, New Hampshire
Laboratory Assistant to Microbiology Department Head, 1993-Present
- Prepare all media and cultures for microbiology classes.
- Order supplies for department, monitor inventory.
- Act as informal tutor, help other students.

DURHAM MEDICAL ASSOCIATES, Durham, NH
Laboratory Technician for four doctors, 1991-1993
- Initiated running of laboratory; organized equipment and materials.
- Ran tests for patients, reported on same-day basis.
- Ordered supplies; maintained inventory.

REFERENCES
Available on request.

- Joan's impressive educational background helps to compensate for her limited work experience.
- Joan's unrelated work experience is omitted.

LAN ADMINISTRATOR

JOAN SMITH
178 Green Street
Albuquerque, NM 87104
(505) 555-5555

CAREER SUMMARY

An experienced professional with expertise in the design and development of multi-user database management systems running on a Local Area Network. Skilled in LAN management and USER training.

BUSINESS EXPERIENCE

JEFFERSON MANUFACTURING CORP., Albuquerque, NM   1988 to Present
Documentation Development Coordinator
Analyze, develop, and maintain application software for engineering LAN. Provide training and user support for all applications to LAN users. Maintain departmental PC workstations including software installation and upgrades.

- Reduced data entry errors and process time by developing an on-line program which allowed program managers to submit model number information.

- Replaced time-consuming daily review board meetings by developing a program which allowed engineers to review and approve model and component changes on-line.

- Developed an on-line program which reduced process time, standardized part usage, and which allowed engineers to build part lists for new products and components.

Computer Systems Analyst   1984-1988
Responsibilities included database management systems analysis and design, workstation maintenance and repair, and LAN management.

- Reduced process time and purchasing errors by developing an on-line program which allowed the purchasing department to track the status of all purchasing invoices.

- Developed a purchase order entry program for the purchasing department which improved data entry speed and reduced the number of data entry errors.

LAFAYETTE, INC., Albuquerque, NM   1979-1984
Engineering Technician III
Prototyped and tested new PC products, drawing schematics, and expediting parts for these new PC products. Designed and coded multi-user database management software for engineering use.

- Expedited the parts for 25 or more telecommunications terminal prototypes. Built, troubleshot, and transferred those prototypes to various departments for testing.

EDUCATION

Associates Electronics Engineering Technology, University of Notre Dame, 1979
Continuing education training courses includes Advanced Digital Electronics, C Language Hands-On Workshop, Visual BASIC Programming, and Structured Analysis and Design Methods.

COMPUTER EXPERIENCE

IBM PC Compatibles, Tape Backup Systems, Local Area Networks, MS-DOS, Lotus 1-2-3, dBase III, DBXL\Quicksilver, Clipper, C Language, Netware 3.11, MS Windows, Visual BASIC, and SQL Language.

- Joan's career summary clearly spells out her area of expertise.
- Resume indicates how Joan contributed to her previous employers.

MARKETING INTERN

JOAN SMITH
178 Green Street
Washington, D.C. 20020
(202) 555-5555

SUMMARY OF QUALIFICATIONS
- Successfully completed finance/marketing internship in Maastricht, the Netherlands.
- Performed market research for new Pinchot Fat Free Cakes.
- Computer Skills: Macintosh; IBM PC and compatible systems.
- Excellent interpersonal and communication skills with verbal, written, presentation, and foreign language translations.
- Multi-lingual: Fluent in Dutch; Conversant in German, French, and Italian.
- Familiar and comfortable with multi-ethnic populations; well traveled and have resided and studied in Amsterdam, Munich, and Rome.
- Demonstrated marketing/public relations, events planning, and fund raising capabilities.

EXPERIENCE

LION BANK   Maastricht, the Netherlands
Finance/Marketing Intern   Spring 1994
Dealt with portfolios, stocks, and bonds. Provided translations. Assisted with research on the Maastricht Treaty and the potential financial ramifications of a unified Europe. Selected as part of the Johns Hopkins-Maastricht Exchange Program as one of only seven students chosen to participate.

BANKS' HEALTH FOODS   Richmond, VA
Market Research Intern   Summer 1993
Assisted with new product research for Pinchot Fat Free Cakes; worked extensively on IBM system.

SWEET BRIAR PRODUCTS, INC.   Annapolis, MD
Research and Development Intern   Summer 1992
Worked for new product development research team.

JOHNS HOPKINS ALUMNI ASSOCIATION   Rockville, MD
Fundraising Coordinator   Summer 1991
Coordinated the procedures and implementation of securing funds for tutoring facility, career and alumni center.

EDUCATION

JOHNS HOPKINS UNIVERSITY   Baltimore, MD
B.S., Political Science; Minor, International Relations Anticipated   Spring 1995

JOHNS HOPKINS-MAASTRICHT   Maastricht, the Netherlands
Student Exchange/Internship   Spring 1994

- Internship experience is valuable for candidates with little job experience, particularly if it corresponds to the position sought.

- Foreign language skills and international exposure, via exchange programs and/or internships, are a valuable asset in today's global market.

NURSE

Joan Smith
178 Green Street
Boston, MA 02115
(617) 555-5555

PROFESSIONAL OBJECTIVE
A position as a professional Registered Nurse in Medical/Surgical, Intensive Care, Emergency Room, and/or Ambulatory arenas.

SUMMARY OF QUALIFICATIONS
- Specialize in ventilators, tracheotomy care, burn patients with extensive dressings, IV therapy.
- Expertise in coordinating discharge planning and home care with doctors, nutritionists, physical therapists, occupational therapists, and social workers; strong on documentation and follow-through.
- Outstanding interpersonal and communication skills.
- Proven written and teaching/demonstration skills for extensive education regarding tracheotomies for in-home care.
- Co-produced educational videos for new staff with specialized information.

PROFESSIONAL EXPERIENCE
1992-Present   **BOSTON HOSPITAL, Boston, MA**   **Staff Nurse, R.N.**
Thoracic Surgery
- Coordinate staffing issues, budget responsibilities, QA monitoring.
- Attend workshops, co-produce and act in educational videos; write working brochures for patients and families.
- Perform primary nursing care; communicate directly with doctors and other health care professionals.
- Participate in extensive post-op care with multiple problems.
- Deal directly with the families regarding hospital policies.

1989-1992   **ST. JOAN'S HOSPITAL, Medfield, MA**   **Professional Registered Nurse**
- As Charge Nurse, provided leadership on 40-bed Medical/Surgical unit with telemetry and provided IV therapy.
- As LPN, employed direct patient care with administration of medications.

EDUCATION
UNIVERSITY OF MASSACHUSETTS, Amherst, MA.
B.S. in Nursing. Graduated 1992 with Nursing GPA of 3.2/4.0.

DEAN JUNIOR COLLEGE, Franklin, MA.
A.S. in Nursing and Applied Science. Graduated 1989.

Major Course Work:
Nursing Research Seminar - Focusing on qualitative, quantitative, and historic research methodology pertaining to nursing.
Community Health Nursing - A study on community and family environment.
Nursing Leadership and Management - An emphasis on nursing administration and budgetary responsibilities.

- Joan's resume is easy and quick to read; only relevant details are included.
- Relevant course work adds depth to Joan's educational background.

CHRIS GREEN
178 Green Street
Berkeley, CA 94720
(415) 555-5555

OBJECTIVE

An OFFICE MANAGEMENT position in the Computer field.

SKILLS PROFILE

- Demonstrated planning, controlling, organizing, and leadership skills. Offer 10+ years of management experience encompassing personnel functions, client relations, and facilities management.
- Human resource skills include determining staffing needs, selecting, hiring, assigning, and supervising.
- Articulate and expressive speaker. Presented numerous well-received client seminars on product features. Conducted intensive on-site training sessions for PMS clients and installation staff.

EXPERIENCE

TOUCHSTONE SYSTEMS, INC. - Berkeley, CA

OFFICE MANAGER   1990-present

Direct and coordinate all aspects of installation, troubleshooting, training, and general customer service operations for the Norwalk branch of TS, INC. Provide all maintenance functions and management of security systems. Administer property management budget with sensitivity to cost control. Respond immediately to building emergencies and implement appropriate course of action. Determine office staffing needs, write and place employment ads, interview and select qualified personnel. Provide orientation and training in company policy and practices, operations, and customer service techniques.

QUARTERMAIN CONTRIBUTORS, INC. - San Diego, CA

BRANCH MANAGER   1988-90

Provided leadership and direction for TS systems installers/trainers outside of the San Diego metropolitan area. Selected, trained, directed, and evaluated the performance of technical support staff, ensuring compliance with the highest possible quality performance standards.

PERCELL ASSOCIATES - Los Angeles, CA

OFFICE MANAGER   1986-88

Managed and oversaw all office functions encompassing the control of annual operating budgets. Sources and negotiated purchasing of cost effective, quality equipment, and supplies.

EDUCATION

BACHELOR OF SCIENCE IN MANAGEMENT, 1986

Pepperdine University, Malibu, CA

Additional courses, workshops and seminars include:

PERSONNEL * WORK TEAMS * BUSINESS WRITING * ORGANIZATION SKILLS

COMPUTER SKILLS

Hardware: IBM * DEC
Communications: PCANYWHERE * QMODEM * PROCOMM
Software: MULTIMATE * PROFESSIONAL WRITE * ONE-WRITE PLUS * WINDOWS * LOTUS 1-2-3

- Joan's job objective is brief and to the point.
- Applicable course work, workshops, and seminars are highlighted.

PARALEGAL

JOAN SMITH
178 Green Street
St. Paul, MN 55104
(612) 555-5555

EXPERIENCE

1989 to   BRODERICK & HOLMES, St. Paul, MN
present   **Corporate Paralegal**, 1984-present

- Solely responsible for ensuring corporate compliance with Minnesota General Laws, meeting and filing requirements for 750 clients.
- Determine interstate corporate business status and handle registration process.
- Extensive contract with State Department of Revenue Compliance Bureau to verify corporate tax standing.
- Draft corporate votes, liquidation and dissolution plans, various agreements, and supporting documents.
- Familiar with UCC financing statements; research liens in connection with corporate acquisitions and financing.
- Supervise, train, and develop administrative staff.
- Determine and collect corporate data for implementation of computerized information system.
- Responsible for organization of new corporations including preparation of articles of organization, drafting of by-laws, and issuance of stock.
- Guide legal interns in department procedure and scheduling.
- Trained on LEXIS and NEXIS legal research systems.

Legal Recruiting Coordinating, 1985-1989

- Aided in recruiting effort in all areas of practice.
- Scheduled interoffice interviews.
- Reviewed attorney and summer associate candidates.
- Coordinated recruiting effort in law schools; contacted placement agencies and established positive working relationships.
- Prepared all materials for hiring committee meetings.

EDUCATION

MACALESTER COLLEGE, St. Paul, MN
Bachelor's Degree in Marketing, 1983
(GPA 3.85)

CARLELTON JUNIOR COLLEGE, Duluth, MN
Associate Degree in Secretarial Sciences, 1978
(GPA 3.75)

Ongoing professional development includes: managing complex financial transactions, organizational structure seminar, and national association for legal placement's annual recruitment conference.

REFERENCES

Furnished upon request.

- Joan's most recent position is outlined in detail.
- Continuing education indicates Joan's ongoing commitment to her career.

PHOTOGRAPHER

JOAN SMITH
178 Green Street
Burlington, VT 05405
(802) 555-5555

OBJECTIVE

A position in photography utilizing my outstanding production and creative skills to improve a company's services and profitability.

KNOWLEDGE/SKILLS

- Black and White film development and printing
- Color Film development and printing, negative, and direct positive processes
- Large format view cameras 4x5; 8x10; Medium format cameras; 35mm equipment
- Studio and location lighting equipment setups
- Special effects, multiple imagery, conventional, and electronic manipulation techniques
- DOS, MAC, Windows Software: Adobe Photoshop, Quark Xpress, Aldus Photostyler, Persuasion, Freehand, Pagemaker, Lotus Freelance, and Paintbrush

EXPERIENCE

Photographer/Assistant   1991-Present

Worked on a variety of location and studio assignments, developed curriculum, and instructed photography classes. Produced superior photo work in a number of venues:

- Articles in National Stamp Collector Magazine
- Photographs for portfolio reproductions and theatrical head shots at Goddard College
- Photo essay for Jake's Fisheries: "A Day Offshore"
- Interpreted layouts, designed and constructed sets for complete on-figure fashion shoots
- Highly skilled at laying out and shooting hard-line advertising

Photographic Assistant   1987-Present

- Frank Zanna, still life, Hubbel Pen, Dom Champagne, 1992-Present
- Jack Camp, still life, Merry Maids, 1991-Present
- Les Meyers, location editorial Goddard College, 1987-1991

ACCOMPLISHMENTS

- Location photography of Men's Swim Team for U.S. Olympic Committee, 1992
- Hard line advertising/marketing brochures/corporate portraits, Kenerson Industries, Burlington, VT, 1991
- Promotional photography for ballet recital, University of Vermont, Burlington, VT, 1991

EDUCATION

Goddard College, Plainfield, VT
Bachelor of Fine Arts in Visual Arts, 1991
Concentration: Photography

- Knowledge/Skills section calls attention to Joan's valuable technical knowledge.
- Specific accomplishments add depth to Joan's experience.

PHYSICAL THERAPIST

JOAN SMITH
178 Green Street
Franklin, IN 46131
(317) 555-5555

PROFESSIONAL OBJECTIVE

A career opportunity in PHYSICAL THERAPY.

CLINICAL EXPERIENCE

MIDWEST MEMORIAL HOSPITAL, Indianapolis, IN
Orthopedic In- and Out-Patient Clinic   1993-1994

- Develop treatment plan for 10 patient caseload.
- Work extensively with chronic pain and cardiac patients.
- Present in-service on hip and knee prostheses.

DEARBORN COUNTY HOSPITAL, Richmond, IN
Cardiac Rehabilitation   1992-1993

- Acted as program coordinator for exercise regimen.
- Provided individualized treatments using modalities, such as ultrasound, electric stimulation, massage therapy, and stretching/strengthening exercises.
- Coordinated aquadynamics program for chronic pain patients.

CINNAMON MOUNTAIN, Mishawaka, IN
Pediatric Rehabilitation   1990-1992

- Coordinated the treatment of amputee children and children with congenital birth defects; created the "Alive with Pride" program that is now functional at thirty national hospitals.
- Encouraged regular exercise by developing child-oriented play program.
- Directed teacher workshops at local elementary schools.

EDUCATIONAL BACKGROUND

INDIANA UNIVERSITY, Bloomington, IN
Bachelor of Science in Physical Therapy, 1990
Awarded Indiana University Scholarship
Course work included Pediatric Therapy and research in the application placement of vibrator and effects of TVR.

GOSHEN COLLEGE, Goshen, IN
Biology Major; Chemistry, French, Calculus, 1987-88

SPECIAL PRACTICUM

INDIANA UNIVERSITY, Bloomington, IN

- Performed independent research evaluating back and shoulder strength of musicians who were suffering from tendinitis or bursitis.
- Presented findings to Physical Therapy Department; later published in the *Indiana Journal of Medicine* (Vol. X, pp. 20-24, August 1992).

- Job descriptions detail Joan's responsibilities and accomplishments.
- Independent research projects, like the special practicum listed here, illustrate Joan's initiative.

PUBLICIST

JOAN SMITH
178 Green Street
Pullman, WA 99164
(509) 555-5555

OBJECTIVE:

Publicist position at ABC Corporation.

EXPERIENCE:

CNBS TELEVISION, "Confrontations," Pullman, WA   1991-Present
Production Assistant
Book main guests and panelists. Generate and research story ideas. Conduct video research. Edit teases for show. Organize all production details for studio tapings. Troubleshoot equipment malfunctions. Monitor lighting and TelePrompter. Coordinate publicity ads in local newspapers.

BARSTOW COMPANY, Seattle, WA   1989-1991
Publicity Assistant
Publicized new books and authors. Assisted in booking media tours (TV, radio and print). Wrote and designed press releases. Fulfilled review copy requests. Conducted galley mailings and general office work.

WNBN-TV, Tacoma, WA   1988-1989
Production Intern
Assisted producers of a live, daily talk show. Researched and generated story ideas. Pre-interviewed possible guests. Logged tapes. Went out on shoots and wrote promotional announcements. Produced five of my own segments for the show.

THE BENEDICT COUNCIL, UNIVERSITY OF WASHINGTON, Seattle, WA 1987-1988
Promotional Assistant
Implemented promotional campaigns for concerts on campus. Wrote and designed promotional advertisements. Initiated student involvement with program.

THE CHERRY HAIKU, INC., Seattle, WA   1986-1987
Art Assistant
Responsible for paste-ups/mechanicals. Operated Photostat camera; coordinated logistics for photo shoots. Participated in "brainstorming" sessions with creative team.

EDUCATION:

UNIVERSITY OF WASHINGTON, Seattle, WA
B.A., Cum Laude May, 1988
Major: Communication
Minor: English

- Resume emphasizes Joan's contributions and achievements and the problems she has solved throughout her career.
- Joan's job objective refers to a specific job opening advertised in a classified advertisement.

JOAN SMITH
178 Green Street
Tallmadge, OH 44278
(216) 555-5555

SUMMARY:

- Recognized for ability to plan, organize, coordinate, and direct successful fundraising programs, volunteer committees, public relations programs, and educational programs.
- Broad knowledge of legislative procedure.
- Extensive volunteer recruiting and training.

EXPERIENCE:

Ohio Association for Multiple Sclerosis, Akron, OH
Public Relations Manager
Fundraising Director (1991-present)

- Served as Consultant to seven chapters in Ohio on campaign problems and activities.
- Organized state-wide and regional campaign meetings and developed fundraising programs.
- Chairperson for Committee for a Healthier Ohio.
- Special assignments included reviewing all state legislation concerning Association for MS and its programs; staffing Legislative Advisory Committee and following through on specific bills; acting as Training Coordinator for five three-day orientation courses held for new employees.

Campaign Director (1989-1991)

- Administered $1 million campaign, including every aspect of fundraising.
- Recruited 40,000 volunteers.
- Wrote campaign letters; ordered all campaign material; staffed Campaign Advisory Committee; coordinated and directed chapter-wide meetings; conducted staff meetings.
- Maintained campaign records; tested new materials and ideas; assisted chapter department heads and the executive director.

National Lung Association, Sandusky, OH
Campaign Director (1986-1989)

- Directed complete direct mail fund raising campaign ($250,000); formulated policy in the areas of scheduling, list building, coding and testing; cooperated with public relations director in developing campaign materials; trained and supervised up to fifty office volunteers.

EDUCATION:

MS degree in Public Relations, 1985 - University of Dayton, Dayton, OH
BA degree in Government, 1981 - Macalester College, St. Paul, MN

- Statistics and dollar figures quantify Joan's accomplishments.
- Job descriptions emphasize Joan's ability to successfully manage and complete projects.

REAL ESTATE BROKER

JOAN SMITH
178 Green Street
Fargo, ND 58102
(701) 555-5555

SKILLS:

- Real Estate Brokers License, North Dakota, 1983
- Closing High-End Sales
- Generating and Developing Prospective Clients
- Developing Sales and Support Networks
- Cold Calling, Telemarketing, Advertising Expertise
- Outstanding Interpersonal and Communications Skills

EXPERIENCE:

SMOOTH MOVES, INC.   **Fargo, ND**
Real Estate Broker   1991 to Present
Sell single, multi-family, and investment residential properties. Develop and utilize sales networks, cold calling, telemarketing, and advertising to generate buyers, sellers, and financiers. Specialist in no-money-down and foreclosure sales. Maintain active troubleshooting and negotiating involvement through closing.

- Originated Client Concerns Division of the company.
- Assisted in increasing market share from 10% to 30%.
- Sold over $2 million in downturned market.

GET OUT OF TOWN, INC.   **Minot, ND**
Real Estate Broker   1988 to 1991
Sales and Rentals of single and multi-family, high end homes and condominiums. Proficient in obtaining difficult to receive financing. Specialist in executive relocations. Adept at handling difficult and out-of-town clients.

- #1 Rental Broker in company history.
- Averaged $1.5 million in sales per year.

CATCH THIS PRODUCTIONS   **Bismarck, ND**
Owner/Operator   1985 to 1987
Founded and operated a musical booking agency, booking nightclubs, talent and tours on a local and nationwide basis. Developed and maintained profitable relationships with nightclubs and talent, as well as a nationwide network of other agents. Negotiated percentages, dates, and details.

BURNS & CLAP   **Bismarck, ND**
Sales Manager   1983 to 1985
Promoted from Rental Broker after 6 months, with added responsibility to motivate Brokers and coordinate marketing and advertising campaigns.

EDUCATION:

COLLEGE OF WOOSTER, Wooster, OH
B.A., Business Management, 1982

- Joan's skills are highlighted in a separate section.
- Bulleted statements highlight Joan's on-the-job achievements.

JOAN SMITH
178 Green Street
Boise, ID 83725
(208) 555-5555

OBJECTIVE

A position in recruiting with a progressive, expanding firm offering growth potential within the organization's structure. Willing to relocate and/or travel.

ACCOMPLISHMENTS

- Established excellent relationships with employment agencies from California to Massachusetts; increased quantity and quality of resumes received by 200%.
- Developed monthly mailer directed to agencies.
- Implemented new administration procedures, increasing clerical productivity by 95% and reducing personnel department overhead by 30%.

EXPERIENCE

<u>Professional Recruiter</u> - TAB/GTK Corporation, Boise, ID
August 1994-present

- Recruit sales and marketing support personnel.
- Plan and execute field recruiting trips to major cities, seminars, career centers, conferences, and universities.
- Design and implement college recruiting programs.
- Establish and maintain working relationship with select employment agencies.
- Prepare statistical reports relating to department expenditures and provide recommendations for eliminating excessive cost and overhead.
- Assist in the development of employee communication programs.

<u>Personnel Manager</u> - Bannen Boot Company, Syracuse, NY
May 1992-August 1994

- Established first complete personnel program including developing all procedures, records, programs, sources of hire, and all administrative functions related to the recruiting and hiring of personnel.
- Established a child care service in-house.
- Worked on human relations problems arising with the introduction of newly established standards and work procedures.
- Developed new employee orientation programs including visual aids and prepared tests.
- Developed and maintained employee recreation program, music and PA system, bulletin boards, etc.

EDUCATION

Syracuse University, School of Communications, Syracuse, MA
BS Degree, Public Relations, 1989. Minor: Sociology.

- Indicating a willingness to relocate and/or travel can be advantageous for a candidate in the field of recruiting.
- Accomplishments section highlights Joan's most impressive achievements.

RESTAURANT MANAGER

Joan Smith
178 Green Street
Waterville, ME 04901
(207) 555-5555

PROFESSIONAL OBJECTIVE
A responsible and challenging position in Restaurant Management.

SUMMARY OF QUALIFICATIONS
- Design and implementation of management systems, administrative policies, and operational procedures.
- Qualified Butcher, Saucier, Baker, and Chef.
- Menu planning and experience with Italian, French, Oriental, Mexican, and Nouvelle American cuisine.
- Hiring/termination, supervising, scheduling, training, evaluating, and motivating professional and support staffs.
- Troubleshooting actual and potential problem areas, and implementing viable solutions that are both profitable and efficient.
- Purchasing food and supplies, and monitoring inventory.
- Knowledge of financial systems and procedures.
- Exceptional interpersonal, customer service, liaison, and follow-through skills.
- Presentation of a positive and professional image.

PROFESSIONAL BACKGROUND
1982-Present   THE TEMPEST, Waterville, ME
                Manager/Chef
- Assisted in the start-up of 200 seat restaurant featuring 120 item menu containing Italian, French, Oriental, Mexican and Nouvelle American cuisine prepared from scratch.
- Standardized recipes, procedures, and systems including written test that all employees must pass.

1981-1982   NO FRILL COUNTRY COOKING, Orono, ME
             Manager Trainee
- Learned all aspects of restaurant management for 250 seat establishment with $125,000 weekly volume.
- Stations included Saute, Fry, Salad, Baking, Hot/Cold Sauces, Portioning, Inventory, Ordering, Scheduling, and Supervision.

EDUCATION
Johnson and Wales, Providence, RI
B.A. Hotel and Restaurant Management, 1980

- Summary of qualifications highlight Joan's leadership and problem-solving skills.
- Numerical figures such as seating capacity, weekly volume, and number of menu items, give a clear picture of Joan's working environment.

JOAN SMITH
178 Green Street
Los Angeles, CA 90035
(310) 555-5555

OBJECTIVE: A **Retail Management** position.

EXPERIENCE:
6/92-Present SPINNER RECORDS CORPORATION, Los Angeles, CA
Manager   5/94-Present
- Operated Spinner's largest volume store (approximately $50,000/week).
- Hire, train, and coordinate a staff of 26.
- Direct sales floor activities.
- Handle all merchandising, inventory control, ordering, cash control, and maintenance functions.
- Coordinate special promotions and events.
- Prepare daily sales reports.
- Interact with corporate personnel at all levels.
- Assist in developing local marketing and advertising strategies.

Assistant Manager   6/92-4/94
- Oversaw full range of retail management responsibilities.
- Assisted in merchandising.
- Opened/closed store; handled customer service complaints and cash control.
- Supervised and motivated employees.

4/90 -5/92 SANTA ANA SHOPS, Santa Ana, CA
Assistant Manager
- Handled hiring, merchandising, and cash control for this small convenience store.
- Supervised 15 employees.
- Opened and closed market.
- Prepared bank deposits and daily sales reports.

ACHIEVEMENTS:
- Won two merchandising display contests.
- Received the "Super Spinner" Sales Award for exceeding sales goals, 1994.

REFERENCES:
Furnished upon request.

- Specific dates of employment (month and year) are ideal for candidates with no gaps in work history.
- Impressive achievements further enhance Joan's qualifications.

SALES ASSISTANT

Joan Smith
178 Green Street
Fort Worth, TX 76112
(817) 555-5555

EXPERIENCE:

1990- REGENCY CORPORATION, Dallas, TX
Present **Sales Assistant:** Act as liaison between customer and sales representative. Provide customer service via telephone. Ascertain order accuracy. Track and expedite orders. Cooperate in team endeavors.

1987-1990 THE MUSIC MAKER, Inc., Houston, TX
Sales Assistant: Coordinated sales efforts of a staff of six for a large musical instruments dealership. Developed and maintained working relationships with manufacturers and customers. Supported top account executives. Maintained open files to ensure greatest customer satisfaction.

1985-1987 CITY OF DALLAS, TREASURERS DEPARTMENT, Dallas, TX
Research Assistant: Assisted in the collection of delinquent real estate, personal property and motor vehicle excise taxes. Matched instrument of taking against daily tax title receipts. Processed petitions of foreclosure for the legal section and title searches.

1984-1985 TRAFFIC AND PARKING DEPARTMENT, Dallas, TX
Senior Claims Investigator: Investigated and expedited claim settlements relating to ticket disputes and information request.

1983-1984 SHERMAN BANK FOR SAVINGS, Sherman, TX
Bank Teller: Interacted with customers, processed all money and check transactions, balanced all transactions at the end of each shift. Operated a Wang Word Processor, CRT and TRW terminal, and developed a working knowledge of money market funds and IRA accounts.

EDUCATION:

Austin College, Sherman, TX
A.S. Business Management, 1983

Texas Institute of Banking
Completed courses in Bank Organization and Business English, 1981

- Joan lists her education towards the bottom of her resume because her practical experience outweighs her degree.
- Reverse chronological format focuses employer's attention on Joan's most current position.

SALES MANAGER

JOAN SMITH
178 Green Street
Providence, RI 02912
(401) 555-5555 (Days)
(401) 444-4444 (Evenings)

CAREER SUMMARY

Sales professional who, for seven years, has solved problems and met customer needs to consistently generate top sales. Acknowledged for pursuit of personal and professional growth through study and application of proven ability to create Win-Win opportunities for all parties involved.

RELEVANT EXPERIENCE

1990-Present

EAGLE TECH, INC.   Providence, RI
Sales Manager

- Marketed and sold engineering solutions and graphic equipment including workstations, terminals, printers, software, and other related peripherals.
- Generated a $350,000 order for color printers from Dublin Aircraft which was a result of business relationships cultivated with key corporate contacts.
- Convinced a major account on value of new terminal even though the required driver was not yet available. Persuaded the account to pressure their software vendor to write the driver for the terminal. Result: Closed a $400,000 sale of 40 terminals.
- Trained and supervised a new service technician to provide sales support. He was subsequently promoted for outstanding performance.
- Recognized as top sales performer in Eastern half of the United States and inducted into "Leaders." Achieved $4.1 million in sales and exceeded quota of $3.6 million.
- Orchestrated sales efforts with the U.S. Navy and a government contractor to implement a war gaming system. Commitment to service with rapid follow-up resulted in sales of $600,000. Anticipate additional sales of at least $1.4 million.

1988-1990

LEONARD FINN CORPORATION   Newport, RI
Territory Manager

- Managed a remote territory while supervising sales and equipment installation in a wide range of companies throughout nine counties.
- Sold conversion from Macintosh system to The National Bank of Rhode Island, producing a sale of $75,000.

1987-1988

PEARSON PROBLEM SOLVERS, INC.   Bristol, RI
Direct Marketer/Manager

- Created and implemented sales plan to promote inventory control system for retailers.

EDUCATION

COLBY COLLEGE, Waterville, ME
B.S., Marketing, 1986

- Career summary accentuates Joan's acquired professional skills and impressive track record.
- Joan's unrelated work experience is omitted.

SOCIAL WORKER

Joan Smith
178 Green Street
Baltimore, MD 21218
(301) 555-5555

PROFESSIONAL EXPERIENCE

1985 to 1994   DEPARTMENT OF DEPENDENT SCHOOLS, Vienna, Austria
Clinical Social Worker, Vienna Center for Education
Provided direct social work services to elementary and high school students and
their families. Member of on-call child psychiatry emergency team. Conducted
parent education groups. Supervised interns and trained school personnel.

1980 to 1984   **Clinical Social Worker**, American School of Vienna
Provided outreach clinical services to American elementary schools in addition to
responsibilities similar to those described above.

FIELD TRAINING

1980 to 1981   ANDREW T. FERRIS CHILDREN'S CLINIC, Baltimore, MD
Second Year Field Placement
Primary duties included diagnostic evaluation and treatment of children,
adolescents, adults and families, and investigation of Care and Protection Petitions
within multidisciplinary team.

Summer   BALTIMORE COMMUNITY CENTER, Baltimore, MD
1980   **Intern**
Responsibilities included: intake, evaluation and treatment of individuals, couples
and families in a medical and social service setting.

1979 to 1980   BALTIMORE JUVENILE COURT CLINIC, Baltimore, MD
First Year Field Placement
Responsibilities included: diagnostic evaluation and treatment of children,
adolescents, adults and families. Participated in multidisciplinary evaluations.

EDUCATION

JOHNS HOPKINS UNIVERSITY, Baltimore, MD
Master of Social Work, 1979

COLBY COLLEGE, Waterville, ME
Bachelor of Psychology/Sociology, Cum Laude, 1975

AFFILIATIONS

- Academy of Certified Social Worker
- International Association of Social Workers

References available upon request

- Job-related affiliations demonstrate Joan's active participation in her field.
- Joan's international work experience adds weight to her qualifications.

SPECIAL NEEDS EDUCATOR

JOAN SMITH
178 Green Street
Salt Lake City, UT 84112
(801) 555-5555

EDUCATION:

University of Wisconsin, Milwaukee, WI
B.S., Education, 1977

Montclair State College, Upper Montclair, NJ
General Curriculum, two years

CREDENTIALS:

Life Language Learning Disabilities, Utah
Learning Disabilities and Emotional Disturbance, K-12, Wisconsin
Teaching Emotionally Handicapped Certificate, New Jersey
Multiple Subject Teaching Credential, K-12, Oregon

EXPERIENCE:

Salt Lake Independent School District, 1988-Present
Valley Middle School, Salt Lake City, UT
Teacher - Self-contained, Severe Emotional Disabilities Classroom

Streaming Meadows Psychiatric Hospital, Summer 1989
Salt Lake City, UT
Ninth Grade Summer School Teacher - Multiple Subjects

Cedar City Independent School District, 1986-1988
Cedar Middle School, Cedar City, UT
Special Education Teacher
Behavior Adjustment Classes for Severely Emotionally Disabled Children
- Participated in Curriculum and Staff Development
- Revised Grade Six Special Education Mathematics Curriculum Guide

Social Vocational Services, 1984-1985
Group Home, Medford, OR
Home Manager
- Supervision, IPP implementation for six autistic children.

Madison Schools, 1982-1984
Madison Grammar School, Madison, WI
Primary Behavior Disorder Teacher, grades 1-3

Milwaukee Public Schools, 1978-1982
Marquette Elementary School, Milwaukee, WI
Continuing Substitute (2nd grade)

- Joan's impressive credentials are accentuated under a separate heading.
- Joan's work history is stated in reverse chronological order, with her most recent employment listed first.

SURGEON

Joan Smith, M.D.
178 Green Street
Providence, RI 02903
(401) 555-5555

EXPERIENCE

PROVIDENCE GENERAL HOSPITAL, Providence, RI
Staff Heart Surgeon
Appointed May, 1988

RESEARCH EXPERIENCE

1989 INSTITUTE OF CHILD CARE, Harvard University, Cambridge, MA
Worked within Department of Developmental Anatomy.
Conducted research on cardiac anatomy and pathology.
Research led to awarding of Master of Science degree in
Medicine.

1988 DEPARTMENT OF ANATOMY, University of Rhode Island,
Kingston, RI
Conducted histochemical research on the urinary tract.

1987 MAXWELL HOSPITAL, Davis, CA
Conducted research on cardiac anatomy, within the Cardiac
Anatomy Laboratory.

1985 CHILDREN'S HOSPITAL, Davis, CA
Conducted part-time research in cardiac pathology.

1982 to STANFORD UNIVERSITY, Stanford, CA
1984 Received general surgical training, at Burnt Oak Hospital,
General Hospital, and Abbey Road Hospital.

1975 to CHILDREN'S HOSPITAL, Pepperdine Medical School, Malibu, CA
1979 Performed research on congenital heart disease, as a
medical student, during elective periods.

EDUCATION

1987 UNIVERSITY OF CALIFORNIA, Davis, CA
1984 STANFORD UNIVERSITY, Stanford, CA
1981 PEPPERDINE UNIVERSITY, Malibu, CA
Doctor of Medicine Degree, M.D.

POST-GRADUATE TRAINING

1985-1987 Surgical Residency: City Hospital, Davis, CA
1982-1984 Surgical Internship: Good Fellow Hospital, Stanford, CA

LICENSURE

Rhode Island #MD-075261-E
Board Eligible: General Surgery/8

- Valuable research experience is highlighted in detail.
- Dates are clearly listed in left margin.

THERAPIST

Joan Smith
178 Green Street
Houma, LA 70363
(504) 555-5555

EXPERIENCE

THERAPIST   1991-Present
Private Practice   Houma, LA
Render quality counseling services to private clientele with varied psychological disorders. Develop rapport and relationships of trust; facilitate clear communication. Assess symptoms and personal information to diagnose problems and devise effective treatment strategies.

- Assess client progress and effectiveness of treatment plans.
- Involve guardians and family members in supporting therapeutic activities.
- Make referrals to specialists or social service organizations as appropriate.
- Maintain knowledge of new developments in the field and applications to personal practice.

COORDINATOR OF PROGRAM SERVICES
COUNSELOR/ADVOCATE   1988-1991
Domestic Violence Services, Inc.   Orono, ME
Provided leadership and management expertise for efficient daily operations of this non-profit organization specializing in counseling and services for victims of domestic violence. Assessed needs and coordinated delivery of information, referrals, advocacy, and counseling.

- Responded appropriately to hot line calls and emergency situations.
- Provided one-on-one counseling to battered women and children.
- Conducted play groups for children living in the shelter as volunteer in 1988.
- Served as Intern Advocate for victims before the Orono Superior court.

EDUCATION

MASTER OF ARTS IN PSYCHOLOGY, 1991
Teacher's college, University of Maine, Orono, ME
Masters Thesis: Impact of Classroom Learning on Students' Behavior

BACHELOR OF ARTS IN PSYCHOLOGY, 1988
Colby College, Waterville, ME

Additional courses, workshops, and seminars:
Identification and Treatment of Trauma and Abuse • Rational Emotive Therapy
CareerPro Leadership Seminar • Group Facilitation • Cultural Diversity
AIDS • Drugs and Alcohol Abuse • Supervision and Management Training
Family Therapy • Battered Woman Syndrome • Women Portrayed in Media

---

- Bullets call attention to Joan's most significant qualifications.
- Joan's strong educational background is emphasized.

TRAVEL AGENT

JOAN SMITH
178 Green Street
Plymouth, MA
(505) 555-5555

OBJECTIVE
A challenging position within the Travel Industry.

SUMMARY OF QUALIFICATIONS
- Ten years of experience acquired during employment and educational training within the travel industry.
- Thorough knowledge of various reservation transactions, including: booking, bursting, ticketing, interfacing with contracted vendors to ensure realization of customer reservation specifications, sales and customer service.
- Competent familiarity with Sabre computer system.
- Proficient in the provision of general office duties.

EXPERIENCE

1990 to Present   **Support Agent**
AS THE CROW FLIES TRAVEL   Plymouth, MA
- Burst tickets and ensure correct formatting of ticket transaction data.
- Book hotel reservations and direct customer package specifications.
- Process ticket transactions via the Sabre computer system.
- Provide sales services and develop sales strategies.
- Respond to customer inquiries for general and package information.

1987 to 1990   **Sales Representative/Accountant**
BUZZWORD TRAVEL   Hyannis, MA
- Extensive accounting tasks in basic bookkeeping.
- Monitored the selling of corporate and leisure accounts.
- Researched and processed credit checks.
- Verified international and domestic fares.

1985 to 1987   **Tour Guide**
SILVER SENTINEL TRAVEL   Provincetown, MA
- Organized tour schedules for international students. Booked local cruises.
- Acted as assistant to company accountant. Performed general bookkeeping duties.

EDUCATION
TRAVEL SCHOOL OF NEW ENGLAND, Springfield, MA, 1985
QUINCY COLLEGE, Quincy, MA, 1984
Completed travel and marketing courses, 1985

- Summary of qualifications clearly spells out Joan's area of expertise.
- Only Joan's relevant educational training is included.

URBAN PLANNER

Joan Smith
178 Green Street
Lansing, MI 48906
(517) 555-5555

PROFESSIONAL EXPERIENCE

DIRECTOR, OFFICE OF ECONOMIC DEVELOPMENT   **Lansing, MI**

1984-Present   *Community Development Group.* Manage $5 million budget. Supervise staff of ten. Develop policy and direction for grant programs. Evaluate activities of non-profit organizations statewide. Initiate new programs in response to identified constituency's needs, and oversee proposal review, grant monitoring and training and technical assistance. Serve as liaison with public and private agencies supporting non-profit community-based organizations.

SPECIAL ASSISTANT TO THE DIRECTOR   **Lansing, MI**

1982-83   *Community Development Group.* Oversaw foundation fundraising, public relations and information referral. Assisted in project development, implementation and administration. Organized training programs for Board and staff.

TECHNICAL ASSISTANCE COORDINATOR   **Lansing, MI**

1980-81   *Community Development Group.* Provided all training and technical assistance as required by agency's contract with Office of Neighborhood Development. Planned and presented seminars for local organizations. Coordinated technical assistance for various community agencies outside Michigan including project areas such as housing development, housing management, commercial development and industrial retention and expansion.

GOVERNOR'S TASK FORCE ON ECONOMIC DEVELOPMENT OF WOMEN
     Lansing, MI

1980   Member of Task Force to make recommendations to Governor concerning assistance to female small-business owners.

EDUCATION

MASTERS IN CITY AND REGIONAL PLANNING
Michigan State University, East Lansing, MI, 1980

BACHELOR OF ARTS
Albion College, Albion, MI, 1976
Major: Geography
Honors: Cum Laude

- Chronological format emphasizes a clear career path.
- Job descriptions stress Joan's accomplishments, instead of simply listing her job responsibilities.

JOAN SMITH
178 Green Street
Minneapolis, MN 55404
(612) 555-5555

OBJECTIVE:
The opportunity to utilize background and experience in National/International Marketing, Sales and Purchasing in a Marketing and Sales or Off-Shore Sourcing position.

PROFESSIONAL EXPERIENCE:
Littleton and Keats, Minneapolis, MN
VICE-PRESIDENT   1990-Present
Background Information: For this $10 million, industry-leading producer of toys and related items manufactured & sold Nationally/Internationally through Toy Stores, Supermarket Chains, as well as Catalogs. Started as Purchasing Manager, assuming additional responsibilities for outside sales, and on basis of outstanding success in the development and handling of key accounts & general operations, advanced to current position of Vice-President in charge of Sales & Product Development.

ACCOMPLISHMENTS INCLUDE:
- Personal Sales over $4 million/year, while managing/working with network of over 46 sales organizations employing 150 sales representatives.
- Managed Development, Sourcing, Manufacturing and Importation of total Doll and Doll Accessory product lines from Far East & Europe. *Reduced cost of manufacture by 15%.*
- Added $350,000 at significant margin to Gross Sales through establishment of new division marketing line of Doll accessories. Developed new fashions projected at $600,000 first year sales.
- Developed new Sales Accounts, through establishment of national rep./distributor organization, from annual sales of $250,000 *to current volume of $850,000.*

Cattail Inc., Buffalo, NY
GENERAL MANAGER   1984-1990
- Supervised 30, including 8 inside & 9 outside sales personnel in the marketing & sales of all product lines, while setting up telemarketing program, developing special promotions, organizing/managing trade show participation, sourcing, and handling new product evaluations.
- Worked closely with 90 major manufacturers' representative organizations or individuals.
- Turned inventory up to 6 times/year.
- Negotiated several exclusive lines with companies responsible for production of over 50% of gross volume.
- Increased sales during this period from $2 million to $4.5 million.

■ Background information on present employers adds weight to Joan's already strong qualifications.

■ Specifically citing the number of employees Joan supervised draws attention to her leadership abilities.

10
Cover Letters

While your resume is a summary of your credentials, your cover letter should essentially be a sales pitch. Your aim is to demonstrate why your skills and your background make a perfect match for the position you're applying for.

The cover letter is not the place to summarize your background—you have already done this on your resume. Remember, employers typically receive hundreds of resumes for each job opening. You must stand out from other job seekers in a positive way.

The best way to distinguish yourself is to highlight one or two of your accomplishments or abilities that show you are an above-average candidate for this position. Stressing only one or two unique attributes will increase your chances of being remembered by the recruiter and getting to the interview stage, where you can elaborate on the rest of your accomplishments.

You can also gain an extra edge by showing that you have some specific knowledge about the company and the industry. This shows that you are genuinely interested in the job you are applying for—and that you are not blindly sending out hundreds of resumes. More importantly, the employer will view your interest as an indication that you are likely to stay with the company for a substantial period of time if you are hired.

WHEN TO SEND A COVER LETTER
Always mail a cover letter with your resume. Even if you are following up an advertisement that reads simply "send resume," be sure to include a cover letter. It is not professional to send out a resume without one.

LENGTH OF THE COVER LETTER
Four short paragraphs (on one page) is the ideal length for a cover letter. A letter any longer than that is unlikely to be read.

PAPER SIZE

Use standard 8-1/2 x 11 inch paper for your cover letter. If you use a smaller size, the correspondence will appear more personal than professional; a larger size would simply look odd.

PAPER COLOR

Like your resume, white and ivory are the only acceptable paper colors for a cover letter.

> "Look at it this way. Your cover letter is more important than your resume itself, since if it doesn't impress the reader, he or she may not even look at your resume."
>
> —Carter Smith, editor
> The *JobBank* series

PAPER QUALITY

As with resumes, standard, inexpensive office paper (20 pound bond) is generally acceptable for most positions. Executive and top-level positions may require more expensive stationery papers such as ivory laid.

PREPRINTED STATIONERY

Unless you're a top-level executive with years of experience, you should avoid using preprinted stationery.

TYPING

Your best options are to use a high-quality office typewriter, a word processor with letter-quality type, or a word processing program on a computer with a letter-quality printer.

However, the quality of the type on your cover letter is not as crucial as it is on your resume. A good, clean home typewriter is a satisfactory alternative for your cover letter. On the other hand, a dot matrix printer or a home typewriter that does not produce clear, crisp letters is unacceptable.

GUIDELINES FOR CONTENT

There is considerably more latitude in what is considered acceptable content for a cover letter than there is for a resume.

However, don't assume that you need not be as careful with your cover letters as your resume—it could cost you valuable opportunities.

Here are some guidelines to help you construct great cover letters:

- Use proper English and avoid abbreviations and slang. Use short sentences and common words.
- Make your letters more interesting by using action verbs such as "designed," "implemented," and "increased," rather than passive verbs like "was," and "did."
- Personalize each letter. Do not send form letters!
- Be sure each letter fits onto a single page. (Actually, the letter should give the appearance of being half a page long.)

THE TEN KEY INGREDIENTS OF SUCCESSFUL COVER LETTERS

1. Return address. Your return address should appear in the top right hand corner, without your name. As a general rule, you should avoid abbreviations in the addresses of your cover letters, although abbreviating the state is increasingly common in all business correspondence.

2. The date. The date should appear two lines beneath your return address on the right hand side of the page. Write out the date; do not use the abbreviated format.

   Example: May 12, 1995

3. The addressee. Always try to find the name and proper title of the addressee before you send out a cover letter. Two lines beneath the date, list the full name of the addressee preceded by Mr. or Ms. (Do not use Miss or Mrs., even if you happen to know the marital status of the addressee). On the next line, list the individual's formal title; on the subsequent line, list the name of the company. This is followed by the company's address, which generally takes two lines. Occasionally, the individual's full title or the company name and address will be very long, and can appear awkward on the usual number of lines allocated. In this case, you may prefer using an extra line.

4. The salutation. The salutation should be typed two lines beneath the company's address. It should begin with "Dear Mr." or "Dear Ms.", followed by the individual's last name and a colon. A colon appears more businesslike than a comma. Even if you have previously spoken with an addressee who has asked to be called by first name, you should never use a first name in the salutation.

5. First paragraph. State immediately and concisely which position you wish to be considered for and what makes you the best candidate for that position. If you are responding to a classified ad, be sure to reference the name of the publication and the date the ad appeared. Keep the first paragraph short and hard-hitting.

   Example: Having majored in Mathematics at Boston University, where I also worked as a research assistant, I am confident that I would make a very successful research trainee in your Economics Research Department.

6. Second paragraph. Detail what you could contribute to this company, and show how your qualifications will benefit this firm. If you're responding to a classified ad, specifically discuss how your skills relate to the job's requirements. Remember, be brief! Few recruiters will read a cover letter longer than half a page.

   Example: In addition to my strong background in mathematics, I also offer significant business experience, having worked in a data processing firm, a bookstore, and a restaurant. I am sure that my courses in statistics and computer programming would prove particularly useful in the position of research trainee.

7. Third paragraph. Describe your interest in the corporation. Subtly emphasize your knowledge about this firm (the result of your research effort) and your fa-

miliarity with the industry. It is common courtesy to act extremely eager to work for any company where you apply for a position.

Example: I am attracted to City Bank by your recent rapid growth and the superior reputation of your Economic Research Department. After studying different commercial banks, I have concluded that City Bank will be in a strong competitive position to benefit from upcoming changes in the industry, such as the phasing out of Regulation Q.

8.   Final paragraph. In the closing paragraph, specifically request an interview. Include your phone number and the hours when you can be reached or mention that you will follow up with a phone call within the next several days to arrange an interview at a mutually convenient time.

It you are responding to a newspaper ad that asks for your salary requirements, you may decide that you would rather discuss such matters at the job offer stage. However, not stating your salary requirements when asked to do so may jeopardize your chances of even getting to an interview. (This is particularly true of entry-level positions). If you decide to state your salary requirements, do so in a range. For example, your cover letter may read, "I seek a starting salary between $18,000 and $22,000."

Example: I would like to interview with you at your earliest convenience. I am best reached between 3:00 and 5:00 P.M. at (617) 555-1483.

9.   The closing. The closing should begin two lines beneath the body of the letter and should be aligned with your return address and the date (toward the right of the page). Keep the closing simple—"Sincerely" suffices. Four lines underneath this, and aligned with the word Sincerely, type in your full name, preferably with a middle name or middle initial.

Sign above your typed name in black ink. Don't forget to sign the letter! As silly as it sounds, people often forget to sign their cover letters. This creates the impression that you don't take care with your work.

10.   The enclosure line. You will help the employer to see you as a meticulous, detail-oriented professional if you include an enclosure line at the bottom of the letter.

DON'T FORGET TO PROOFREAD!

It's very easy to make mistakes on your cover letters, particularly when you're writing many in succession. But it is also very easy for a corporate recruiter to reject out of hand any cover letter that contains errors. Why hire someone who doesn't appear to take care with such an important piece of correspondence? As with your resume, you must proofread your cover letters carefully—and have a friend proofread them as well.

AVOID MESSY CORRECTIONS

Try to avoid using correction fluid or making any messy corrections. It's always a better idea to take the time to retype the letter perfectly.

RESPONSE TO A CLASSIFIED ADVERTISEMENT

178 Green Street
Waterbury, CT 06708
(205) 555-5555

December 5, 1995

Pat Cummings
General Manager
Any Corporation
1140 Main Street
Chicago, IL 60605

Dear Mr. Cummings:

My interest in the position of Masonry Supply Manager (*New York Post*, November 30) has prompted me to forward my resume for your review and consideration.

During the past ten years, my experience has been concentrated in the masonry and plastering products supply industry with a building materials firm. During my six years as General Manager, I took an old line business, which had undergone several years of poor management, and reversed the trend. I upgraded the firm's image, and customer and vendor relations, which subsequently increased the dollar volume and bottom line profits by 300%.

I am presently looking for a position where my experience will make a positive contribution to the start-up or continuing profitable operation of a business in which I am so well experienced.

I will contact you in a few days to arrange a meeting for further discussion. In the interim, should you require additional information, I may be reached at (203) 555-5555 between 9 A.M. and 5 P.M.

Sincerely,

Joan Smith

Joan Smith

Enc. resume

RESPONSE TO A CLASSIFIED ADVERTISEMENT

178 Green Street
Knoke, IA 50553
(515) 555-5555

February 3, 1995

Pat Cummings
Senior Marketing Manager
Any Corporation
1140 Main Street
Chicago, IL 60605

Dear Ms. Cummings:

In response to your advertisement in the February 1 edition of the *New York Times* for an International Purchasing Agent, I would like to submit my application for your consideration.

As you can see, my qualifications match those you seek:

YOU REQUIRE:	I OFFER:
A college degree	A Bachelor's degree in English from Long Island University
Fluency in Italian and French	Fluency in Italian, German, and French
Office experience	Experience as a receptionist at a busy accounting firm
Typing skills	Accurate typing at 60 WPM
Willingness to travel	Willingness to travel

I feel that I am well qualified for this position and can make a significant contribution to Any Corporation. My salary requirement is negotiable.

I would welcome the opportunity for a personal interview with you at your convenience.

Sincerely,

Joan Smith

Joan Smith

Enc. resume

"COLD" COVER LETTER TO A POTENTIAL EMPLOYER

178 Green Street
Manchester, NH 03104
(603) 555-5555

July 31, 1995

Pat Cummings
Human Resources Director
Any Bank
1140 Main Street
Chicago, IL 60605

Dear Mr. Cummings:

Having majored in mathematics at Rice University, where I also worked as a Research Assistant, I am confident that I would make a successful addition to your Economics Research Department.

In addition to my strong background in mathematics, I offer significant business experience, having worked in a data processing firm, a bookstore, and a restaurant. I am sure that my courses in statistics and computer programming would prove particularly useful in an entry-level position.

I am attracted to Any Bank by your recent rapid growth and the superior reputation of your Economic Research Department. After studying different commercial banks, I have concluded that Any Bank will be in a strong competitive position to benefit from upcoming changes in the industry, such as the phasing out of Regulation X.

I would like to interview with you at your earliest convenience.

Sincerely,

Joan Smith

Joan Smith

Enc. resume

"COLD" COVER LETTER TO A POTENTIAL EMPLOYER

178 Green Street
Emmans, PA 18049

July 18, 1995

Pat Cummings
Chief Executive Officer
Any Corporation
1140 Main Street
Chicago, IL 60605

Dear Mr. Cummings:

My interest in continuing my professional career in the health care field has prompted me to submit my resume for your review.

For fifteen years, I have dedicated myself to providing quality health care in medical staff support in diverse areas including patient care, orientation, and training of volunteer staffs, inventory control, facilities reorganization, and service coordination.

The enclosed resume summarizes my background and experience in these and other areas. I will be glad to furnish you with any additional information during a personal interview or by phone at (215) 555-5555.

Thank you for your time. I look forward to your response.

Sincerely,

Joan Smith

Joan Smith

Enc. resume

"COLD" COVER LETTER TO AN EMPLOYMENT AGENCY

178 Green Street
Salamanca, NY 14779
(716) 555-5555

May 13, 1995

Pat Cummings
Director
Any Corporation
1140 Main Street
Chicago, IL 60605

Dear Mr. Cummings:

In July of this year, I will be permanently relocating to the Chicago area. I am forwarding the attached resume for your evaluation because of my desire to contribute my comprehensive experience in real estate/property management to a locally-based company.

I have two years of direct experience involving all aspects in the management of 275 apartments and four commercial units in three buildings. My diverse responsibilities include a range of activities from advertising and promotion of apartments to competitive analysis of rate structures.

My experience also includes contractor negotiations, liaison with government and service agencies, personnel relations, financial management, and other functions basic to effective management of complex properties.

If you know of any company with a current need for a bright, outgoing property manager with an orientation to sales, please do not hesitate to contact me.

Thank you for your consideration.

Sincerely,

Joan Smith

Joan Smith

Enc. resume

"COLD" COVER LETTER TO AN EXECUTIVE RECRUITER

178 Green Street
Erwin, TN 37650
(615) 555-5555

October 30, 1995

Pat Cummings
Executive Recruiter
Any Corporation
1140 Main Street
Chicago, IL 60605

Dear Mr. Cummings:

During the past fifteen years, I have held senior-level positions ranging from Senior Consultant with a CPA firm, where I specialized in Corporate Financial Planning, to my current job as Chief Financial Officer.

Although I am presently involved in interesting and challenging projects, I am considering a change, preferably to a firm that seeks a high-energy, self-starter for its management team. I have established a fine track record in financial and strategic planning which has produced high-profit results and encompassed:

- Multimillion dollar improvement in cash flow
- Reduction in operating costs and increased profitability of a rapid growth service organization ($15 million to $25 million within two years)
- Profit and business planning, financial evaluation, and long-range financial forecasting for a $150 million group of operating companies
- Negotiation for public and private funding totaling $25 million

My salary requirement is in the $100,000–$120,000 range with appropriate benefits. I would be willing to relocate for the right opportunity.

If it appears that my qualifications meet the needs of one of your clients, I would be happy to further discuss my background with either you or the client. I will be contacting your office in the near future to determine the status of my application.

Sincerely,

Joan Smith

Joan Smith

Enc. business profile

NETWORKING LETTER

178 Green Street
Wolfeboro, NH 03894
(603) 555-5555

June 27, 1995

Pat Cummings
Principal
Any School
140 Main Street
Chicago, IL 60605

Dear Ms. Cummings:

It was a pleasure to speak with you a few months ago at the "National Women in Education Convention" in Boston.

As you may recall, I was then working as an English teacher at Amos Academy in Manchester, New Hampshire. However, due to extensive cuts in the faculty budget and my own lack of seniority, my position has been eliminated.

During our conversation, I remember you mentioned your search for an English teacher for grades 7 and 8. I realize that much time has passed, and this position has more than likely been filled. However, I was hoping that you may know of a similar opening within your district or that you may have some suggestions as to others with whom it might be beneficial for me to speak.

I can be reached at the telephone number listed above. I would appreciate any leads you could give me.

Again, I very much enjoyed our conversation.

Sincerely,

Joan Smith

Joan Smith

Enc. resume

NETWORKING LETTER

178 Green Street
Savage, MT 59262
(406) 555-5555

September 28, 1995

Pat Cummings
Telecommunications Consultant
Any Corporation
1140 Main Street
Chicago, IL 60605

Dear Ms. Cummings:

Several years ago I was a classmate of your son Dustin at the University of Miami. When I bumped into him last week in Billings, Montana, of all places, he informed me that you deal closely with several leading specialists in the telecommunications field and suggested I contact you immediately.

I am interested in joining a company where I can contribute strong skills and education in communications. I offer:

- Bachelor of Arts degree in Communication Science
- Familiarity with all areas of marketing, public relations, and advertising
- One year experience as a Promotions Intern at a radio station
- Fluency in German

I would greatly appreciate any advice and/or referrals you might be able to give me. I will call you in a few days to follow up.

Thank you for your time.

Sincerely,

Joan Smith

Joan Smith

Enc. resume

FOLLOW-UP LETTER (After a Telephone Conversation)

178 Green Street
Boise, ID 83725
(208) 555-5555

August 3, 1995

Pat Cummings
Vice-President
Any Corporation
1140 Main Street
Chicago, IL 60605

Dear Ms. Cummings:

I am forwarding my resume in regards to the opening we discussed in your Marketing Department.

Although I am currently employed in a management position, I am interested in a career change, especially one where I can combine a thorough knowledge of boating with my sales, marketing, and communication skills. I am an imaginative, well organized self-starter with strong interest in boating. As a semi-professional sailboat racer, I twice won national honors and participated in the races at Cape Cod. In addition, I have made lasting contacts with owners and officials.

After you have had the chance to review my resume, please contact me so that we can further discuss the possibility of my joining your staff. I am confident that my business background and knowledge of boats will enable me to have a favorable impact on both your sales and image.

Thank you for your attention, and I look forward to speaking with you again to learn more about this opportunity.

Sincerely yours,

Joan Smith

Joan Smith

Enc. resume

FOLLOW-UP LETTER *(After an Informational Interview)*

178 Green Street
Toast, NC 27049
(919) 555-5555

July 26, 1995

Pat Cummings
Associate Professor of Psychology
Any Corporation
1140 Main Street
Chicago, IL 60605

Dear Ms. Cummings:

It was a pleasure seeing you again today. I appreciate the time you found in your busy schedule to meet with me.

It was interesting to learn about the use of interactive toys and models in child psychology. I have already been to the library to borrow the book by Leonard Finn that you recommended so highly. I am looking forward to reading about his ideas on child's play before the latency period.

I will be contacting Mr. Finn within the next few days to set up an appointment. I will let you know how everything is progressing after I have met him.

Again, thank you for your assistance. You will hear from me soon.

Sincerely,

Joan Smith

Joan Smith

FOLLOW-UP LETTER (After a Job Interview)

178 Green Street
Chicago, IL 60605
(312) 555-5555

August 5, 1995

Pat Cummings
Vice-President of Operations
Any Corporation
1140 Main Street
Chicago, IL 60605

Dear Mr. Cummings:

I greatly enjoyed our meeting yesterday. I would like to reiterate my interest in Any Corporation's opening for a Materials Manager.

As I explained during our conversation, I feel confident that my qualifications match the requirements of the position. I offer twelve years experience working as Manager of Warehousing and Distribution and as Senior Buyer for a large metropolitan hospital. Briefly, my accomplishments include:

Reducing expenditures of all in-house medical and non-medical supplies by 20% through cost-effective negotiations, purchasing, and control.

Automating inventories which increased efficiency and decreased costly errors, thus saving over $10,000 annually.

Designing a functional warehouse layout which effectively reduced the selection and distribution process for warehoused materials and provided more stringent controls.

Reducing shrinkage, damage, and obsolescence of inventory by 33%.

Thank you for the time and courtesy you and your associates extended to me. I will look forward to hearing from you.

Sincerely,

Joan Smith

Joan Smith

FOLLOW-UP LETTER *(After a Job Interview)*

178 Green Street
Flat, AK 99584

November 19, 1995

Pat Cummings
President
Any Corporation
1140 Main Street
Chicago, IL 60605

Dear Ms. Cummings:

It was a pleasure meeting you today. I appreciate you taking the time from your hectic schedule to speak with me about your opening for an Executive Assistant.

The position is exciting and seems to encompass a diversity of responsibilities. I believe that with my experience and skills, I would be able to contribute significantly to your business.

I look forward to hearing from you in the near future. If you need further information, please feel free to call me.

Sincerely,

Joan Smith

Joan Smith
(907) 555-5555

REJECTION OF OFFER LETTER

178 Green Street
Winterthur, DE 19735
(302) 555-5555

February 14, 1995

Pat Cummings
Vice-President, Research and Development
Any Corporation
1140 Main Street
Chicago, IL 60605

Dear Mr. Cummings:

Thank you for taking the time to meet with me on Friday to discuss the opportunities for employment within your Research and Development Department.

While I appreciate your generous offer, I have decided to withdraw from consideration for the position. I have accepted a position elsewhere which I feel is better suited to my long-term needs.

Again, many thanks for your time. I wish you the best of luck in your future endeavors at Any Corporation.

Sincerely,

Joan Smith

Joan Smith

ACCEPTANCE LETTER

178 Green Street
Green Bay, WI 54301

March 17, 1995

Pat Cummings

Any Corporation
President
1140 Main Street
Chicago, IL 60605

Dear Mr. Cummings:

I have received your letter of March 10, and am thrilled to accept Any Corporation's offer to become your new Labor Relations Specialist.

I have formally resigned from the Blackwell Company, and will be relocating to the Chicago area within the next four weeks. I will be able to better pinpoint an exact starting date within the next few days.

You will be hearing from me again soon to finalize the remaining details of our agreement.

Thank you again for giving me this opportunity to become a part of the Any Corporation team. If you have any questions or require additional information, please do not hesitate to call me at (414) 555-5555.

Sincerely,

Joan Smith

Joan Smith

THANK YOU LETTER *(After Hire)*

178 Green Street
El Segundo, CA 90245
(310) 555-5555

December 22, 1995

Pat Cummings
Software Engineer
Any Corporation
1140 Main Street
Chicago, IL 60605

Dear Mr. Cummings:

I am pleased to inform you that my job search has come to a successful conclusion. Yesterday, I was offered a position with L. GWA PO Inc., a Japanese software conglomerate that has recently opened a branch office in Los Angeles. I am delighted to be able to participate once again in the fast-paced world of computer technology.

I would like to extend my warmest thanks to you for your kindness and encouragement during my job search. The next time you visit LA, please be sure to let me know.

Happy holidays and best wishes for the new year!

Sincerely,

Joan Smith

Joan Smith

Part III
The Job Hunt

11

Planning Your Job-search Campaign

No matter how terrific it may be, your resume alone will not land you a job. You will need a comprehensive and well-defined plan in order to job hunt effectively. A plan will help you keep up the vigorous pace of the job-search process and keep you from becoming frustrated or unmotivated. It will also enable you to pace yourself and monitor your progress against predetermined goals. If your plan is not an effective one, you will be able to see problems more clearly and tackle them head-on by changing direction or using different techniques.

Your job-search plan should incorporate a number of different job-finding methods. Decide which of the strategies described in chapter 12 you want to try first. If you plan to pursue classified ads, decide which newspapers are worth monitoring. If you want to contact companies directly, find out which sources of company listings will best suit your needs. If you plan on networking (which experts strongly recommend), make a list of people you plan on contacting first.

Predict how much time you are going to spend pursuing these different avenues and set up a specific weekly schedule for yourself. It's important not to overlook this step; it will help you be more productive and make it more difficult to fall behind.

GETTING ORGANIZED

Organization will make your job search more efficient and less stressful. Obviously, you should try to keep your desk or work area free of clutter. Make a to-do list at the beginning of each day and try to accomplish each of your goals by the end of that day. Also, use an organizer notebook that includes a pen and a daily calendar for recording appointments. Be sure to take it with you to interviews.

It's also important to create a chart or similar system that shows where and to whom you've sent your resume. Use it to track whether or not companies have responded and when and if you need to follow up with a phone call.

Oversized index cards are another useful way to organize your job search. Keep each contact's name, position, company, address, telephone number, contact method, follow-up date, status, and other important details on individual cards for quick and easy reference. If you are responding to an advertisement in a newspaper, clip the ad and paste it onto the card, along with the name of the newspaper and the date. If an employer or networking contact gives you her business card, you can staple it to an index card, and jot down any other pertinent information as well. Keep all of your cards in a index card box in alphabetical order for easy reference.

HOW LONG SHOULD YOUR JOB SEARCH TAKE?

As you may have already discovered, finding a job is not easy. It takes a lot of energy and a tremendous amount of effort. Current statistics show that the average job search lasts approximately one week for every $2,000 of income sought. For example, if your goal is a position that pays in the $30,000 range, your search will take approximately 15 weeks. However, this statistic and others like it obscure one very important fact: you are the person who ultimately controls what kind of job you end up with and how long it takes to find it.

If you are like most job hunters, you will have to contact several hundred companies before you find the right job. If you put tremendous effort into your job search and contact many companies each week, you will probably get a job much sooner than someone who is only searching casually and sending out one or two resumes a week.

> "Job searching takes three to six (really six to nine) months, so sign up for a course or two. Be prepared for the realities, develop time frame strategies, and plan for "meaningful" alternatives. Taking a class or two (through a community college or seminar series) can be the best investment you'll make."
>
> —Burton Nadler, Director of Career Services
> University of the Pacific

JOB HUNTING FULL-TIME

Ideally, for the first few months of your job search, you should try to look for a job full-time. If you're able to afford this luxury, be sure to work from a vigorous, intense job-search plan that allows you to invest a minimum of 40 hours per week.

Vary your activities a little bit from day to day—otherwise your job search may quickly become tedious. For example, every Sunday you could look through the classified ads and determine which jobs are appropriate for you. On Monday, follow up on these ads by sending out your resume and cover letter and making some phone calls. For the rest of the week, you could spend your time doing other things besides following up on specific job openings. On Tuesday, for instance, you might decide to focus on contacting companies directly. On Wednesday, you could do more research to find listings of other companies to contact. Thursday and Friday might be spent networking, as you try to set up appointments to meet with people and develop more contacts.

Every few weeks you should evaluate your progress and fine-tune your search accordingly. If you find that, after putting in a great deal of effort over a period of several months, you aren't even close to getting a job, then it's probably time to reconsider your options. Are the job-search methods you've chosen working well for you? Are you spending too much time responding to newspaper ads and not enough time networking and "cold" contacting? Could you be more aggressive in your job search? (See chapter 15 for advice on how to jump-start a stalled job search.)

The key to an effective job-search campaign is knowing when to persist in the current direction that your job hunt is taking and when to give up what you're doing and start over. It isn't easy. Often, talking with other job hunters and knowing the current state of the job market in your industry of interest will help you to draw this fine line.

JOB HUNTING WHILE YOU'RE STILL EMPLOYED

Looking for a new job while you're still employed can be a sticky situation. Time, or the lack thereof, can be a major problem and you may find yourself feeling more than a bit overwhelmed. Also, there is the very real concern that your current employer will find out that you're looking for a new job before you're ready to tell her. But there are ways to maximize time and minimize stress during your job search.

First, set aside blocks of your days and/or evenings for job hunting. You may choose to bag your lunch and spend your lunch hour making networking calls or following up on resumes you've sent out. Plan to spend several hours on weeknights and on Saturdays mailing out resumes and tracking down job leads. Whatever schedule you decide upon, try to stick to it the best you can.

Executive recruiters and employment agencies that don't charge job hunters a fee may be particularly helpful to the employed job seeker. Not only will they do the footwork for you, but they can help you uncover job leads you may not otherwise be able to find.

There is also a wide range of services that can help you save time by handling some tasks while you're at work, such as a telephone answering service or a resume service that mails out your resume to job leads you supply. These services can be extremely useful to the harried job hunter, but some are not what they seem. Be an informed consumer and shop wisely.

Organization will also play a key role in the success and the length of your job search. It may be worth your while to reread the section on getting organized at the beginning of this chapter.

Of course, time management and organization are probably not your only concerns. You may worry that you'll be found out by your current employer or wonder about the ethical issues involved. To dispel any concerns you may have, you should not feel obligated to inform your current employer that you are job searching until you are ready to give your notice. Revealing this information too soon may very well cost you your job. Remember, employers would rather lose you at their convenience rather than at your own.

To ensure that your job hunt is kept quiet, you should never tell any of your co-workers or colleagues of your plans. This may sound obvious, but it's a mistake that's too often made—at the expense of the job seeker. Also you may choose to head your resume with a phrase like, "Confidential resume of . . . " or make some similar mention of confidentiality in your cover letter. Most recruiters will understand and honor this request for discretion. Ask recruiters not to contact you at work but instead leave a message on your home answering machine, which you can check regularly during the day. Sometimes, though, recruiters will overlook such a request and contact you at work anyway. If you find this happening to you, you may choose to use your voicemail rather than routing your calls through the receptionist.

It's important for job hunters to view their situation realistically. The days when employees dedicated their entire careers to a single employer are long gone. It is to be expected that people will change jobs several times during their career, and it would be foolish to leave a current position without having something else lined up. So if you have a misdirected sense of guilt, you shouldn't. Channel that energy into your job-search efforts instead.

LONG-DISTANCE JOB HUNTING

As if finding a job isn't tough enough, long-distance job hunting can be very difficult. There are several steps you can take to make this transition as smooth as possible. First, call or write your new city's Chamber of Commerce to get information on the city's major employers. Subscribe to a local newspaper and sign up with local employment agencies. Inform your networking contacts of your plans and ask them for any leads or suggestions they can give you in this new location. Do they know of anyone who works in that area who can give you suggestions? Also, be sure to check with your national trade or professional association. Most large associations offer members access to a national network. Contact the national office for a list of chapters in your new city.

If you are relocating to a new city because your spouse has been transferred, be sure to ask your spouse's company about spouse relocation assistance. Some larger companies may offer free career counseling and other job-hunting services to you. If your spouse's employer does not offer this service, consider contacting a career counseling center for guidance. You may be able to negotiate with your future employer to pay the center's fees.

PLANNING YOUR FINANCES

In addition to being stressful, looking for a new job can be costly. Expenses relating to your job hunt, in addition to everyday living expenses, can amount to a formidable sum in the face of a reduced income. Following are some guidelines to help you make this aspect of your job search somewhat smoother.

First of all, if you are laid off, you should know that most companies offer one week's to one month's severance pay for every year of service. Get a written copy of your company's policy. Immediately file for unemployment benefits and, if you can afford it, extend your health insurance. Some larger companies will also offer outplacement services to help employees in their transition to another job. Find out if your company offers any such assistance.

Next, assess your financial fitness. Make a detailed list of all your expenses, separating them into three categories: priority one, two and three. Priority one expenses should include the bare essentials such as rent/mortgage, utilities, groceries, and car payment. Be sure to figure job-search expenses in your priority one list. Priority two expenses should include important but not necessarily essential items such as credit card bills (which can be paid at a later date), home maintenance, and automotive maintenance. Priority three expenses should include more frivolous items that can be sacrificed temporarily, such as cable television, magazine subscriptions, leisure activities, and miscellaneous luxury purchases. Total your estimated expenses in each of these three categories.

Now, make a detailed list of your income and assets. This should include any income from part-time, temporary, and free-lance work, unemployment insurance, severance pay, savings, investments, spouse's income, and alimony.

If you estimate that it will take you six months to find a new job (not a bad measure for today's market), multiply the total of your priority one expenses by six and subtract it from your current income and/or savings for that same period of time. You may find that some budgeting is in order. Perhaps you can cut down or eliminate some of those priority two and three expenses. Determine what is absolutely essential and what can be sacrificed for the time being.

You may also decide to write your creditors to request a reduced payment schedule in light of your employment situation. This may not always be possible, and it can affect your credit rating. But many creditors, when given a choice between receiving a partial payment or no payment at all, will agree to work out an acceptable plan with you. Be sure to ask your creditors to help preserve your good credit rating.

You should also know that some job-hunting expenses are tax deductible if you are looking for a new position in your current line of work. (Unfortunately, no tax relief is available if you switch careers or if you are a first-time job seeker.) All expenses associated with job hunting are generally deductible, including resume typing, printing, postage, telephone costs, travel costs, and employment agency fees. If your new job is at least 50 miles further from your home than your old job was, you will also be able to deduct up to $3,000 of your total moving expenses. Of course, you'll need to accurately document all your expenses so be sure to save all your receipts.

To generate additional income for yourself during this time, consider taking on part-time, free-lance, or temporary work. You may choose to borrow against your life insurance or retirement policy, if you have one, or accept a loan from a friend or relative.

Now that you've determined how much money you have and how much you'll need, establish a realistic budget. It should be very detailed and laid out on paper. Be sure to monitor your budget on a regular basis so you don't suddenly find yourself overwhelmed by a financial predicament that may otherwise have been avoided.

12

The Best and Worst Ways to Find Jobs

You may be surprised to learn that some of the most popular job-search methods are quite unsuccessful for most of the people who use them. In this chapter you'll have a chance to take a look at the real value of the services and techniques at your disposal.

EMPLOYMENT AGENCIES

Employment agencies are commissioned by employers to find qualified candidates for job openings. However, you should know that the agency's main responsibility is to meet the needs of the employer—not to find a suitable job for you.

This is not to say that you should rule them out altogether. There are employment agencies that specialize in specific industries or industry functions which can be useful for experienced professionals. However, employment agencies are not a good choice for entry-level job seekers. They often try to steer inexperienced candidates in a direction they're not interested in and often place them in clerical positions.

If you decide to register with an agency, your best bet is to find one that is recommended by a friend or associate. Barring that, you can find names of agencies in *The JobBank Guide to Employment Services* (Bob Adams, Inc., 1994) found in your local public library, or by contacting the following:

> National Association of Personnel Services (NAPS)
> 3133 Mount Vernon Avenue
> Alexandria, VA 22305
> (703) 684-0180

Be aware, though, that there are an increasing number of bogus employment service firms, usually advertising in newspaper and magazine ads. These companies promise even inexperienced job seekers top salaries in exciting careers—all for a sizable fee. Others use expensive 900 numbers that job seekers are encouraged to call. Unfortunately, most people find out too late that the jobs they are promised don't exist.

As a general rule, most legitimate employment agencies will never guarantee you a job and will not seek payment until after you've been placed. Even so, you should check every agency you're interested in with your local chapter of the Better Business Bureau. Find out if it is licensed and has been in business for a reasonable amount of time. Have any valid complaints been registered against the agency recently? Has the firm been responsive to these complaints?

Then, if all checks out with the BBB, call the firm to find out if it specializes in your area of expertise and how it will go about marketing you. If you are asked to sign a contract, have an attorney look at it first. Find out who will pay the agency's fee. You should avoid any firms that are not company "fee paid."

After you have selected a few agencies (three to five is best), send them your resume and cover letter. Make a follow-up phone call after you've sent your resume and try to schedule an interview. Be prepared to be asked to take a battery of tests on the day of your interview.

Above all, though, do not expect too much. Only a small percentage of all professional, managerial, and executive jobs are listed with these agencies, so they are not a terrific source of opportunities. Use them as an addition to your job search campaign, but focus your efforts on other, more promising methods.

EXECUTIVE SEARCH FIRMS

Also known as headhunters, these firms are somewhat similar to professional employment agencies. They seek out and screen candidates for high-paying executive and managerial positions and are paid by the employer. Unlike employment agencies, they typically approach viable candidates directly, rather than waiting for candidates to approach them. Many prefer to deal with already employed candidates and will not accept "blind" resumes from job hunters.

These organizations are not licensed, so if you decide to go with an executive search firm, make sure it has a solid reputation. You can find names of search firms in *The JobBank Guide to Employment Services* or by contacting the following:

> Association of Executive Search Consultants (AESC)
> 230 Park Avenue, Suite 1549
> New York, NY 10169
> (212) 949-9556
>
> American Management Association (AMA)
> Management Services Department
> 135 West 50th Street
> New York, NY 10020
> (212) 586-8100

As with employment agencies, do not let an executive search firm become a critical element of your job search campaign—no matter how encouraging it may sound. Continue to actively seek out your own opportunities and keep all of your options open.

> "There are actually two types of job searches. A reactive search involves reacting to postings, want ads and recruiting activities. A proactive search is goal-directed, involving networking and contacting organizations related to a field of interest. Too often job seekers limit themselves to reactive efforts."
>
> —Burton Nadler, Director of Career Services
> University of the Pacific

TEMPORARY AGENCIES

Temporary or "temp" agencies (such as Kelly Services and Manpower) can be a viable option for some job seekers. Usually these agencies specialize in clerical and support work but it's becoming increasingly common to find temporary assignments in other areas like accounting, computer programming, and management consulting.

Working on temporary assignment will provide you with additional income during your job search and will add experience to your resume. It may also provide valuable business contacts or lead to job opportunities.

You can find temporary agencies listed in the Yellow Pages. Send your resume and cover letter and later call and try to schedule an interview. You should be prepared to be asked to take a battery of tests on the day of your interview.

NEWSPAPER CLASSIFIED ADS

Contrary to popular belief, newspaper classified ads are not a good source of opportunities for job hunters. Few people find jobs this way, although many spend a tremendous amount of time and effort poring through newspaper after newspaper.

According to career development consultant Charles Logue, less than 3% of all job openings are advertised in classified ads. Worse, so many applicants respond to these ads that the competition is extremely fierce. Even if your qualifications are good, your chances of getting an interview are not. If you plan on using classified ads, be sure to focus only a small portion of your job search efforts in this direction.

BLIND ADS

"Blind ads" are newspaper advertisements that don't identify the employer. Job seekers are usually instructed to send their resumes to a post office box number. Although they may seem suspicious, blind ads can be a source of legitimate job opportunities. A firm may choose to run a blind advertisement because it may not wish to be deluged with phone calls or it may be trying to replace someone who hasn't been terminated yet.

You should be aware, though, that blind ads are sometimes used for deceitful purposes, such as selling employment marketing services and sexually harassing unsuspecting job hunters. The best advice is to trust your instincts and don't allow yourself to be put in a situation that makes you feel uncomfortable.

PUBLIC EMPLOYMENT SERVICE

Your state employment service, sometimes called the Job Service, has about 1,700 local offices (also called employment service centers) nationwide, which provide job placement assistance and career counseling. With so many white collar workers out of work, these agencies are doing more and more to accommodate professional and managerial job hunters. Check your local phone book for the office nearest you.

JOB COUNSELING SERVICES

The job counseling services offered by your city or town are another useful option. You can find them listed in your local phone book or by writing:

> National Board for Certified Counselors (NBCC)
> 3D Terrace Way
> Greensboro, NC 27403
> (910) 547-0607

You may also wish to consult *The JobBank Guide to Employment Services*, which lists career counseling services as well as executive search firms, employment agencies, and temporary help services located throughout the United States.

> "Job seekers who are looking for 'anything' often find 'nothing'. An inability to say what type of job you want is the most common reason for a prolonged job search. Being open limits you to posted opportunities (want ads, search firms, career fairs). Being focused, not boxed in, allows for proactive, goal-directed efforts and enhances networking."
>
> —Burton Nadler, Director of Career Services
> University of the Pacific

NON-PROFIT AGENCIES

It may be worthwhile to find out what services are provided by non-profit agencies in your local community. Many of these organizations offer counseling, career development, and job placement services to specific groups such as women and minorities. Also, try contacting the national organizations below for information on career planning, job training, or public policy support.

For Women:

U.S. Department of Labor
Women's Bureau
200 Constitution Avenue NW
Washington, DC 20210
(202) 212-6652

Wider Opportunities for Women (WOW)
1325 G Street NW
Lower Level
Washington, DC 20005
(202) 638-3143

For Minorities:

National Association for the Advancement of Colored People (NAACP)
Attn: Job Services
4805 Mount Hope Drive
Baltimore, MD 21215-3197
(410) 358-8900

National Urban League
Employment Department
500 E. 62nd Street
New York, NY 10021
(212) 310-9000

National Urban League
Washington Operations
1111 14th Street NW
6th Floor
Washington, DC 20005
(202) 898-1604

For the Blind:

Job Opportunities for the Blind Program
National Federation for the Blind
1800 Johnson Street
Baltimore, MD 21230
(800) 638-7518

For the Physically Challenged:

President's Committee on Employment
of People with Disabilities
1331 F Street NW
Third Floor
Washington, DC 20004
(202) 376-6200

COLLEGE CAREER CENTERS

If you're a recent college grad, your school's career center is a great place for you to start your job search. Your college career center can help you identify and evaluate your interests, work values, and skills. Most offer workshops on topics like job-search strategy, resume writing, letter writing, and effective interviewing, or job fairs for meeting with prospective employers. Yours should also have a career resource library where you can find job leads and an alumni network to help you get started on networking.

Even if you've long since graduated, your college's career center may be able to provide you with valuable networking contacts. You should call to find out if your alma mater offers this or other services to alumni.

ELECTRONIC DATA BASES

Electronic data bases compile information on job seekers to be scanned and searched by hiring companies. They may be the new wave for job seekers of the future, but right now they are primarily used by college students and recent grads, often with limited results.

These services usually charge between $30 and $50 to list your resume for one year. If you decide to go this route, be sure to make it only one small part of your job search plan.

DIRECT CONTACT

One of the best ways to find a job is by direct contact. Direct contact means introducing yourself to potential employers, usually by way of a resume and cover letter, without a prior referral. This type of "cold contact" can be very effective if done the right way. Chapter 13 explains just how to do this.

NETWORKING

Another excellent method of finding work is through networking, a strategy that focuses primarily on developing a network of "insider" contacts. This is a great approach to use even if you don't have any professional contacts. Networking takes many forms; with a little skill and a lot of effort, it can be a very productive tool for you. Chapter 14 takes you through the networking process step by step.

13
Contacting Companies Directly

Direct contact (also called "cold contact") means making a professional, personal approach to a select group of companies. Done well, it can be an excellent method for most job seekers, leading to many opportunities and possibly job offers. However, if you're an experienced professional looking for a high-level managerial or executive spot, you may find that this approach does not work well for you. If you find that this is the case, your best bet will probably be networking (see chapter 14).

THE BEST COMPANIES TO CONTACT

One of the most common mistakes that job hunters make is focusing their search on very large, Fortune 500-type companies. Despite the fact that most of these giants are dramatically downsizing their work force, big corporations still look good to many, who flood human resources departments with resumes. According to a recent article in *Fortune*, IBM receives about one million resumes a year!

But don't give up hope! There are countless midsize companies with anywhere from 100 to 1,000 employees where the competition is much less fierce. These companies are large enough to have a number of job openings at any given time. In fact, experts predict that as many as one-third of all new jobs will be created by midsize firms over the next two years. At the same time, these companies are small enough that they are often overlooked by other job hunters, meaning there will be less competition for job openings.

But the best source of job opportunities today is small companies—those with 100 or less employees. A recent Dun and Bradstreet report predicts small companies will be responsible for almost 80% of the 2.1 million new jobs created in America this year. These companies are not very visible to the general public, meaning that there will generally be less competition for job openings. An additional advantage is that most smaller firms offer significant room for career growth. There are drawbacks, though: small companies generally offer less job security than midsize firms and fewer employee benefits.

DO YOUR HOMEWORK

If you are trying to enter a new field, your first order of business is to do a little background research. Find out the current trends in the industry and become familiar with names of the major and up-and-coming players. Your industry's trade journal and informational interviews are two terrific ways to find this kind of "insider" information. Check your local library for *The Encyclopedia of Business Information Sources* or *Predicasts F&S Index* to identify publications in your field of interest.

If you're a veteran of the field you're looking in, make sure that you keep up with current industry trends by talking with your associates, attending your professional association's functions, and reading your industry's trade journals.

WHAT TO LOOK FOR

Now you should be ready to look for information about individual employers. But rather than going into great detail in your search at this point, you should be trying to find out only basic information about many different companies, including:

- Company name, address, phone, and fax number.
- Names and job titles of key contacts.
- Is the company privately or publicly held?
- What are its products and/or services?
- What is the year of incorporation?
- How many employees does the company have?

Plan on doing further, more detailed research later on as you start to schedule interviews. (See chapter 16 for more on this).

"Reference librarians are the most underutilized, and best job search support persons."

—Burton Nadler, Director of Career Services
University of the Pacific

WHERE TO FIND IT

Where can you find this kind information about potential employers?

One good place to start is the *JobBank* books, a series of employment directories listing almost all companies with 50 or more employees in larger cities and metropolitan areas in the U.S. Each *JobBank* provides up-to-date information including key contacts, common positions the company hires for, educational backgrounds sought, and fringe benefits offered. There is also a section on that particular region's economic outlook and addresses of professional associations, Chambers of Commerce, and executive search and job placement agencies in that region.

You can find the following *JobBank* books at your local bookstore:

Atlanta; Boston; Carolina; Chicago; Dallas/Fort Worth; Denver; Detroit; Florida; Houston; Los Angeles; Minneapolis/St. Paul; New York; Ohio; Philadelphia; Phoenix; San Francisco; Seattle; St. Louis; Tennessee; and Washington D.C.

There are many other resources you can use to find listings of companies, most of which can be found at your local library. Ask the reference librarian to help you locate the many directories available that list basic information about companies in your field of interest. Be sure not to overlook these great tools:

- Dun and Bradstreet's *Million Dollar Directory* is a good place to begin your research. It lists approximately 160,000 companies that are both publicly and privately held and is updated annually.

- *Standard & Poor's Register of Corporations* lists fewer companies than the *Million Dollar Directory* (about 45,000) but provides valuable biographical information on thousands of company officials.

- *Corporate Technology Directory* (Corporate Technology Information Services) focuses on the products produced by approximately 35,000 companies. This is a great resource for job seekers interested in high-tech industries, including computers, biotechnology, environmental engineering, chemical and pharmaceutical, and transportation.

- *Personnel Executives Contactbook* (Gale Research) lists key personnel and other contacts at 30,000 publicly and privately held companies and government agencies.

- *The National JobBank* (Bob Adams, Inc.) lists key contacts at over 17,000 small and large companies. It includes information on common positions filled and educational backgrounds desired and is updated annually.

- *Directory of Human Resources Executives* (Hunt-Scanlon) names human resource executives and provides information on number of employees and area of specialization of 5,000 public and private companies.

- *Directory of Corporate Affiliations* (National Register) is one of the few places where you can find information on a company's divisions and subsidiaries. This particular book lists information on approximately 4,000 parent companies.

Many of these resources can also be found on CD ROM at your library. These "books on disk" are easy to use and can save you a lot of time. They are often attached to printers so you can print the information you need. Usually, libraries will provide free access to CD ROM databases.

Also, don't overlook the countless industry-specific directories that are available, such as *Dunn's Directory of Service Companies, Martindale-Hubbell Law Directory*, and *Standard Directory of Advertisers*. These are a terrific place to find potential employers and often include information on professional associations and industry trends. Ask your reference librarian for help in identifying the directories that specialize in your field of interest.

THINK BIG

As a general rule, you should always *try* to contact a department head or president of any company you consider working for. This will probably be easier to do at smaller companies where the president of the company herself may be directly involved in the hiring process.

However, as you apply to larger and larger companies, you will find yourself more and more often bumped back to the personnel office. If this happens to you, try to contact a key decision-maker within personnel.

The first step you should take in contacting a company directly is to send out your resume, personalized cover letter, and a self-addressed stamped envelope. The letter should be addressed to a specific person; if you are not sure who you should send it to, call the company and ask, making sure to get the correct spelling of the contact's name. You should further personalize each letter by including a reference to something you know about that particular company (presumably through your research). This can make all the difference between getting an interview and getting passed over.

THE 60-SECOND PITCH

Approximately one week after you have sent your letter to a key decision-maker, you should follow up with a phone call. Don't simply ask if your resume has been received—this can be frustrating to employers who are inundated with hundreds of resumes and probably won't get the response you're hoping for. A better approach is to state that you've sent your resume and explain, in 60 seconds or less, why you think you're the best candidate for the position. I call this the "60-second pitch."

Your 60-second pitch should be a clear and concise summary about yourself. It should include three important elements:

1. What kind of work you do (or want to do)
2. What your strongest skills and accomplishments are
3. What kind of position you are seeking

> "Don't try to be something you're not. You can't sell a [product] you don't know."
>
> —Stacey Slaughter Miller,
> *National Business Employment Weekly*

Your resume is probably the best and easiest place to find this information. One communications professional used her resume to create her 60-second pitch:

"Hello. My name is Elaine O'Connor. I'm a production assistant with a B.A. in Communications and three years of solid broadcasting and public relations background. I have extensive experience developing and researching topics, pre-interviewing guests, and producing on-location video tapings.

"I've been watching your station for some time now and I've been impressed with your innovative approach and your fast growth. I recently sent you my resume and was wondering if you anticipate any openings that might be appropriate for someone with my experience?"

Mary, a mom who was returning to a full-time position when her daughter began the first grade, also had a terrific 60-second pitch:

"My name is Mary Johnson. I sent you my resume last week and I'd like to take a moment to introduce myself. I've been working part-time as an accounts receivable supervisor for the past five years and have expertise in payables, receivables, and credit. I'm looking for a full-time accounting position.

I read the article about your firm's recent expansion in last Sunday's business section and think that we might make a great match. Do you have a few minutes?"

As you can see, tailoring your pitch to the needs of each particular employer will make your 60-second pitch stronger. At the same time, you should memorize the "core" of your pitch—the part about your qualifications that you will recite to every potential employer. This will help you feel more confident and sound more natural. Also be sure to speak slowly and clearly.

If you are invited to an interview after you've "pitched" yourself to the employer, great! If not, don't let it end there! Ask if there are any particular qualifications that she is looking for in a candidate. Is there anything else you can do or any additional information that you can send (writing samples, clippings, a portfolio) to help the employer make her decision? Even if she says no, that your resume is sufficient, she may be impressed by your interest and enthusiasm.

Then, if you have not already done so, specifically ask the employer if she would have a few minutes to meet with you. If that doesn't work, ask if she knows anyone who might be interested in speaking with someone with your qualifications. If you are unable to arrange an interview or get a referral, ask the employer if she would mind if you called back in three to four weeks. The goal is to get a positive result from the phone call—whether it's an interview or simply a scrap of job-hunting advice. Don't give up too easily, but be professional and courteous at all times.

GETTING PAST GATEKEEPERS

Gatekeepers are those receptionists, assistants, and other workers who try to screen all calls, making sure only the most important ones go through to the top. You should expect to encounter many gatekeepers throughout your job search—and how you handle them can make a big difference in your campaign.

If your call is screened by a gatekeeper, don't request a call in return unless the contact will recognize your name. Simply give your name and ask when it's best to call back. Call again the next day at the time he or she suggested. Keep calling once a day for at least five days before you change tactics.

Another alternative is to try asking for your contact by her first name. You could say, for example, "This is Susan Thomas. Is Sharon in?" If you say this with an air of confidence and authority, you might just get through.

If you're asked what the call is about, try saying that you've been in correspondence with Sharon and she's expecting your call (if you sent your resume and cover letter, mentioning that you'd be calling). If you're pressed to be more specific, you can say, "I would like Sharon's expertise on a sales and marketing issue." Or use an implied referral, "I was just talking with John Barker at ACME Industries about something that might interest Sharon. Would you put me through, please?"

Whatever approach you choose to take, never say that your call is personal—this sends up a red flag to most gatekeepers and will hurt your chances of getting through.

If none of these approaches work, try calling when the gatekeeper is least likely to be there—before or after hours and during lunch. Employers will often answer their own phone during off hours.

Another technique that works well is to call the office of the president and say something like, "Hi. I don't think I really need to speak with the president—I'm just trying to find out who's in charge of sales and marketing. Could you help me with that?" Then be sure to thank the person and jot down his or her full name. Then you can get past that person's gatekeeper by saying something like, "Bill Warner in the president's office suggested I speak with Sharon Rice. Is she in?"

If none of these suggestions work for you, as a last resort you should ask for the gatekeeper's help. You could say, "Joe, I've been trying to reach your boss for some time now and I haven't had much luck. Do you have any suggestions on how I might be more effective?" A sincere and polite request for help will often either get you through to your contact or at least win a useful bit of advice.

If you've exhausted all of these techniques and feel as if you'll never get through, don't waste your time. Simply move on to other, more promising contacts and opportunities.

CONTACTING THE SAME FIRM TWICE

One approach that can be very effective is calling some of the firms you contacted a few months previously. This shows that you are genuinely interested in the firm and will certainly make you stand out in the contact's mind. You could say something like:

> "My name is Rosemary Brandenburg and I contacted your firm several months ago about an entry-level position in advertising. I've been talking with other firms and I'm very much committed to this industry. I recently saw your firm mentioned in the local newspaper, and I'm more convinced than ever that your company is a terrific place to work.
>
> "I feel I have a lot to offer you and I'd like for you to reconsider my application."

The technique works especially well when you contact firms you interviewed with. Only a fraction of those applying for a position get to the interview stage; if you were one of them, the firm was obviously impressed with your qualifications. Chances are good that you would still be considered for another position at that company.

You don't have to telephone, of course; you might prefer to write a letter. On the following page is a sample letter you could send to a company that interviewed you but did not offer you a position.

Sample Letter for Contacting the Same Firm Twice

81 Sandypine Road
Joppa, Maryland 20707
(301) 555-5555

October 27, 1995

Pat Cummings
Personnel Manager
Any Corporation
1140 Main Street
Chicago, IL 60605

Dear Ms. Cummings:

As you may recall, I interviewed with you back in March for an advertising assistant position. I very much enjoyed meeting with you and was impressed by your organization.

I realize that you have filled that particular opening, but I am contacting you now because I am still quite interested in obtaining a position with Any Corporation. Perhaps you have an appropriate position available currently or anticipate an opening soon.

In case you no longer have my resume on file, I am enclosing another copy for your consideration. As you can see, I graduated from Colgate University this past May with a Bachelor of Science degree in Marketing. In addition to my degree, I have experience working in both marketing and sales.

I would like to be considered for any appropriate job openings that may arise. I may be reached at the above listed phone number between 9:00 A.M. and 5:00 P.M. for an interview at your convenience. Again, thank you for your time.

Sincerely,

Joan Smith

Joan Smith

Enc. resume

DON'T GIVE UP!

Cold contact is challenging and often frustrating. But no matter how frustrated you may become, it's important to be polite to your contacts (and their gatekeepers!) at all times. Like anyone else, they will be more willing to help out a professional, friendly caller than someone who sounds frustrated or unpleasant.

Job searching is not easy for anyone. If you go into it expecting some rejection, it will be easier to take when it happens. This is when attitude becomes crucial. If you're optimistic and you believe in yourself, you have the most important ingredients of a successful job search.

14

Networking Your Way to a Job

Networking is the most effective of all job-hunting tools. In fact, experts indicate that as many as 86% of all jobs are found through networking. This chapter is designed to dispel the mystery and confusion that often surrounds this job search method. As you read on, you will see that networking is not just for people with lots of professional experience. It can work for anyone—even people with few or no contacts in the business world.

OVERCOMING HESITATION

If you feel hesitant about networking, you're not alone. Many job seekers mistakenly think that networking is somehow degrading or manipulative. They suspect that networking really means pestering strangers for a job and begging for scraps of help and sympathy. They opt not to use this important tool and end up needlessly limiting their opportunities.

The problem is that these people don't understand what networking really is. Networking means letting people you know—personally and professionally—that you are looking for a job. You simply ask them to keep you in mind if they hear of any appropriate openings or know anyone who might need someone with your skills.

It will probably feel awkward at first, but with practice you'll feel much more comfortable and confident making calls. Keep in mind that this is a time-honored practice—in fact, it's how most job seekers get jobs. And, once you find the right job, you can "give something back" by lending a hand to other networking job seekers.

> "If you can get the courage to make the first networking call, you'll find out it's not really as scary as you thought."
>
> —Stacey Slaughter Miller
> *National Business Employment Weekly*

PRESENT YOURSELF AS AN INDUSTRY "INSIDER"

One of the secrets of networking is knowing what you want—or at least appearing to know what you want. For instance, if you are trying to break into a field where you don't have any experience, tell your networking contacts that you are interested in the industry they work in and show them that you are knowledgeable about that industry. This way, you will be perceived more or less as an "industry insider." Better yet, if you can cite some work experience in that industry and a referral, people will be interested in talking with you.

So—how do you start? Keep up to date with your industry of choice by reading its trade journals. Check your local library for *The Encyclopedia of Business Information Sources* or *Predicasts F&S Index* to identify publications in your field of interest. Be sure to read your industry's publications on a regular basis.

In addition, you should keep an eye out for information about your chosen industry that appears in the mainstream media: your daily newspaper, magazines like *Time* and *Business Week*, news broadcasts, books, and other sources.

TRACKING DOWN LEADS

Who should you contact? Obviously, if you have experience in your industry of choice, you need only leaf through your rolodex and call up some of your already established contacts. But how do you network if you don't already have prior experience and contacts?

The answer is simple: start with the people you already know. Friends, relatives, neighbors, your doctor, your hairdresser—even your plumber can be a source of important business contacts. These people might not work in the industry you're interested in, but they may know someone you should contact. Someone who knows someone who . . . you get the idea.

At first, you might not think you have many contacts at your disposal—but if you think carefully you'll realize you do. Let's say that there are 30 people you can initially contact, but none of them work in the industry you're interested in. They may, as a group, know 60 people who do work in that industry, work in a related industry, or are in a position to know someone who works in the industry. That's a lot of people.

But don't stop there. Contact the people you know on a professional or academic basis, such as former teachers, past employers and co-workers, and established business contacts. Find out if your college, graduate, or prep school offers networking services for alumni. If not, they will probably have an alumni directory that you can use.

Consider joining a professional organization. If you don't know the associations in your field and their locations and publications, consult the *Encyclopedia of Associations* or *National Trade and Professional Associations of the United States*. Your local library should have these books on hand.

Lastly, you should make a point of getting out and talking to people in your industry through informational interviews, seminars, even at social events—anywhere you would might expect to find "insiders."

These organizations can be a great source of networking contacts and valuable job-hunting information:

9 to 5, National Association of Working Women focuses on helping working women in job-related areas, publishes books and pamphlets, and offers a hot line for job-hunting advice. For more information, call (800) 522-0925 or write 9 to 5, 614 Superior Avenue NW, Suite 852, Cleveland, OH 44113.

American Association of Retired Persons (AARP) provides legislative advocacy, research, informative programs, and community services to people over 50. Of particular value is AARP's publication *Returning to the Job Market: A Woman's Guide to Employment Planning.* For more information, write AARP, 601 E Street NW, Washington, DC 20049.

American Business Women's Association publishes a magazine with career advice. For more information, call, (816) 361-6621 or write American Business Women's Association, 9100 Ward Parkway, Kansas City, MO 64114.

Exec-U-Net is a nationwide association of managers and professionals based in Norwalk, Connecticut. Exec-U-Net's newsletter, published every two weeks, provides an average of 250 job leads, none of which have been advertised. Listings come from the groups's 2,000 members, search firms, and companies. For more information, call (800) 637-3126.

Forty Plus Club is a national organization that provides a range of career services to unemployed executives over 40 years old. To find the club nearest you, call (212) 233-6086 or write Forty Plus of New York, Inc., 15 Park Row, New York, NY 10038.

National Association for Female Executives (NAFE). This is a network of 250,000 women across the country in all professions at all levels. NAFE offers a handful of benefits including career development seminars, career guides and resume services, legal and financial services, group insurance coverage, and subscription to their high-quality bimonthly magazine. For more information, call (800) 634-6233 or write NAFE, 30 Irving Place, New York, NY 10003.

National Association for Women in Careers provides support, networking contacts, and skills development services. For more information, call (708) 358-4965 or write National Association for Women in Careers, 675 North Court, Suite 200, Palatine, IL 60067.

Women Work! The National Network for Women's Employment lends a helping hand to those women trying to make the transition from home to the workplace, offering career counseling, training and technical assistance, job placement, support groups, financial management assistance, and tuition assistance. For more information, call (202) 467-6346 or write Women Work! The National Network for Women's Employment, 1625 K Street NW, Suite 300, Washington, DC 20006.

National Federation of Business and Professional Women's Clubs is an advocacy group for working women with over 100,000 members. It operates the Clairol scholarship program and offers grants to women. For more information, call (202) 293-1100 or write BPW/USA, 2012 Massachusetts Avenue NW, Washington, DC 20036.

Older Women's League publishes career information on job discrimination, counseling, and other career information. For more information, call (202) 783-6686 or write Older Women's League, 666 11th Street NW, Suite 700, Washington, DC 20001.

Wider Opportunities for Women (WOW) sponsors the Women's Work Force Network, a national network of 350 employment programs and advocates. For more information, call (202) 638-3143 or write Wider Opportunities for Women (WOW), 1325 G Street NW, Lower Level, Washington, DC 20005.

WHAT SHOULD I SAY AND DO?

First you should tell your contact a little bit about your qualifications and what kind of job you're looking for. If the contact is not someone who already knows you well, you should cite the name of the person who referred you and then introduce yourself with your 60-second pitch (as described in chapter 13). Be sure at some point to ask the contact if she knows of anyone who might be looking for someone with your qualifications. Then ask for the name of anyone who might know anyone looking for someone with your qualifications.

If the conversation is going well, you may decide to ask your contact if she would have a few minutes to meet with you. If you are unable to arrange an interview or get a referral, ask the employer if she would mind if you called back in three to four weeks.

> *"Helen Barrett? Hello, my name is Leslie Pellham. Jason Randall at Computing Associates was telling me yesterday about your company's recent innovations in applications and recommended that I speak with you. Do you have a minute to talk with me? Great.*
>
> *"I've been a programmer for 11 years at PC Systems and I'm looking for a change of pace. I was hoping you could tell me a little more about your firm and the qualities you look for in job candidates.*
>
> *"I see. Well, I have a thorough knowledge of COBOL, Pascal, Fortran, and C++ in a windows and DOS environment. I also have experience in information mapping. It sounds as if we might make a good match. Could I come in and meet with you for a few minutes at your convenience?"*

Now, if Helen agrees, Leslie should schedule an appointment and thank her for her time. If Helen declines, however, Leslie should politely persist:

> *"Oh, I understand—you don't have any openings right now. Is there someone you can think of who might be looking for somebody with my qualifications? Also, I'd like to send you my resume anyway in case a position opens up in the near future."*

If Helen says she can't think of anyone, Leslie should ask her for a referral. Chances are that her polite persistence will pay off and she'll come away with at least one new contact.

NETWORKING FOR WOMEN ENTERING A NEW FIELD

If you are trying to enter a new field, it's a good idea to ask your contacts for information about the industry in general and about their particular position. Are there any specific qualifications or training that makes some candidates more competitive than others? Tell each of your contacts a little bit about your situation and ask for advice.

This is how Janet, a recent college graduate, "pitched" herself to a potential employer:

> *"Mr. Silva, my name is Janet Philipps and my uncle, Joe Adams, suggested that I call you. I've just graduated from City University with a degree in English. I've been working part-time as a bank teller for two years and I very much want to pursue a career as a loan officer. I realize that you may not have any openings at this time but I was hoping that you would be able to meet with me for a few minutes to discuss the banking industry."*

Mr. Silva then says he's very busy and he doesn't have the time to meet with Janet. Janet politely persists:

"I understand that you're busy—that's why I'll only ask for one more minute of your time. As you know, I have some part-time work experience in banking. Are there any other specific qualifications or training that you could recommend that would help me get a job as a loan officer?"

Mr. Silva then gives Janet some advice on how to get a job in the banking industry.

"Thank you for that suggestion—I'm sure it will be very helpful. Now, would you be able to refer me to someone who might be looking for someone with my qualifications?"

If Mr. Silva says no, Janet should ask if he knows anyone who might know anyone looking for a job in the banking industry. The point is to get at least one referral or job lead from each contact.

"Thank you for referring me to Ms. Lehman at Center Bank—I'll be sure to call her today. In the meantime, though, could I send you my resume for your files? Great. Thank you again for all your help. By the way, Uncle Joe says hello!"

THE INFORMATIONAL INTERVIEW

Informational interviews are an important way of building your network and can lead to valuable information and opportunities.

If you tell a contact that all you want is advice, though, make sure you mean it. Never approach an informational interview as though it were a job interview—just stick to gathering information and leads and see what happens.

"Always sound upbeat and cheerful. People like to help others who are positive and confident."

—Susan Zitron, President
Career Management Services

Tell your contact right away that all you would like is to learn more about the industry or company in question, and that you'll be the one asking all the questions. Also, unless it's specifically requested, sending your resume to someone you'd like to meet for an informational interview will probably give the wrong impression.

"My name is Janet Philipps and David Silva suggested I call you. I've just graduated from City University with a degree in English and I'm interested in beginning a career as a loan officer.

"I know that you may not have any openings at this time, but I would like to come by and talk with you for a couple of minutes about the opportunities that might be available in banking."

Sometimes an employer will mistake your intentions and tell you that she has no jobs available. If this happens, you can say something like:

"I understand that you might not have any openings right now, but I'd like to have a chance to meet with you for a couple of minutes anyway, just to discuss the banking industry in this city and the opportunities one might expect at those places that might be hiring. Would this be possible?"

You might find that the straightforward approach sometimes works better:

"My name is Janet Philipps and David Silva suggested I call you. I've just graduated from City University with a degree in English and I'm interested in beginning a career as a loan officer.

"I assure you I won't ask you for a job, but I was hoping that you would be able to meet with me briefly to discuss the banking industry."

Now that you've scheduled an informational interview, make sure that you're prepared to take the lead. After all, you're the one doing the interviewing—not vice versa. Have some specific questions ready, such as:

- How did you get started in this business?
- What do you like most about your job, your company, and your industry?
- What do you dislike most about your job, your company, and your industry?
- What would you say are the current career opportunities for someone with my qualifications in the industry?
- What are the basic requirements for an entry-level position in the industry?
- Is there a trade association or a trade publication that might aid me in my job search?
- Where do you see the industry heading in the near future?
- What advice would you give to someone looking for a job in the industry?
- Is there anything else I should know about the industry?
- Do you know of anyone who might be looking for someone with my qualifications?
- Do you know of anyone who might know of anyone looking for someone with my qualifications?

SEND A THANK-YOU LETTER
If a networking contact has been particularly helpful to you, by all means send a thank-you note. Not only is this courteous, it keeps your contacts current.

MORE NETWORKING?
Go back and call once again those people you already contacted for leads several months ago. You could say something like:

"As you may remember, we spoke several months ago about my interest in a career in banking. I was hoping that you might know of some other people who might be looking for someone with my qualifications."

You may be pleasantly surprised. It's not uncommon to catch a contact in a different frame of mind and learn of someone new. Or perhaps your contact has met someone in your industry of interest since you last spoke.

> "The biggest mistake people make is thinking networking is like hunting for business. Networking is really more like farming. You have to spend time and effort cultivating before it pays off."
> —Ivan Misner
> Business Network International

WHEN YOU RUN INTO TROUBLE . . .

Don't be discouraged if you don't get a tremendous response at first—remember, job hunting is very much a waiting game. But if you find yourself running into trouble (as most job seekers do at some point), the next chapter should help you keep your head above water . . .

15
Troubleshooting in Tough Times

After several months of job searching, you may find that you've made less progress than you had hoped or you may be having trouble making ends meet. If you are an older job candidate or among the physically challenged, you may be facing issues that only add to the usual difficulties associated with job hunting. This chapter is designed to help you get through the toughest job search challenges.

JUMP-STARTING A STALLED SEARCH

If you find, as time goes by, that you aren't getting very far in your job search, ask yourself the following questions:

- Are you qualified for the position you are seeking? There's nothing wrong with aiming high, but being unrealistic is another story. Ask yourself if you're ruling out jobs that you're better qualified for. If you're not sure if your goals are realistic, seek the opinion of a career counselor or someone who works in the particular job or industry you're seeking.

- Are there any courses, training sessions, or seminars that could help make you a more competitive candidate for the job you are seeking? This can be a great way to give yourself an extra edge and to impress potential employers with your initiative and determination.

- Does your resume look sharp? A poor resume can destroy the chances of even the most qualified applicants.

- Is your cover letter personalized? If your cover letter resembles a form letter, you're greatly minimizing your chances of getting an interview. True, personalized letters take more time and effort, but you'll probably get better results sending out one personalized letter than five form letters.

- How many personalized cover letters and resumes are you sending out each week? Could you send out more? Remember, with every company you contact, you increase your chances of finding a job.

- Are you following up every resume with a phone call? Many job seekers try to avoid making phone calls, assuming that employers will contact them. Following up your resume and cover letter with a phone call is very important and will dramatically increase your chances of getting an interview.

- Are you contacting companies that are smaller and less known? Are you using all the different job-search methods outlined in chapter 12?

- Are you networking as much as you can? Networking—or lack of it—can make or break a job-search campaign. Make sure it doesn't break yours.

If you think that you might be having trouble finding a job because you have no experience in a particular field, consider doing an internship while you are job hunting. Although internships are often not paid, they can provide valuable experience, numerous business contacts, and sometimes even job opportunities. For some fields, free-lance work can also be a good way to get your foot in the door.

If you are getting a number of interviews but no job offers, chances are you need to work on your interview performance. Remember, you should consider not only what you say during job interviews but how you are saying it. Do you present yourself as mature and confident or are you nervous and unsure of your answers? If you need to improve your interview skills, you might want to read *Knock 'em Dead: The Ultimate Job Seeker's Handbook* by Martin Yate (Bob Adams, Inc., 1994). This exceptional book will help you improve your interview skills dramatically and increase your chances of winning job offers.

Whatever you do, practice. Practice interviewing with different relatives and friends—and even in the mirror! The more you do it, the more confident you'll feel and the better you'll present yourself during your actual interviews.

If you've tried all of these suggestions and still nothing is working, you may want to consider broadening the scope of your job search. This could mean focusing on a broader job category or an additional industry. Another option is to look for a job in a number of different regions of the country, particularly where jobs in your area of interest are more plentiful. Of course, long distance job hunting is more difficult, but it is now almost commonplace. (See chapter 11 for more on long-distance job hunting.)

> "If you have been unemployed for a significant period of time, you might find it fiscally prudent to accept that less-than-perfect job. That's okay. By the same token, there is a big difference between settling for less than your dreams and making the wrong job your life's work. If circumstances force you to take a temporary detour from your ultimate career goal, give an honest day's work for an honest day's pay and continue to pursue other opportunities."
>
> —Martin Yate, author
> *Knock 'em Dead: The Ultimate Job Seeker's Handbook*

COPING WITH STRESS

After several months of tedious job searching, you'll probably be dealing with your share of stress. Stress is the result of feeling a lack of control. If you're feeling a bit overwhelmed, what you need to do is empower yourself by seizing control in small ways. Straighten up your desk and organize your job-hunting information. Get rid of unneccessary clutter. Continue to write a daily to-do list, and be sure you cross the items off the list as the day progresses.

It's important to stick to a regular sleeping and eating schedule. Be sure to shower and get dressed every morning, even if you're not going out. You should exercise daily, even if it's only a 20 minute walk. It will boost your mood, keep you fit and energetic, and provide a break from job hunting.

How you feel about your situation and about yourself will also have a significant impact on the outcome of your job search. View your career transition as a positive change, a chance to learn and grow. Like all change, it's bound to be a bit frightening, but recognize and accept that it isn't unusual or wrong to experience stress, fear, and occasional panic during your job search. Learning to recognize and relieve stress will make your job search easier and ultimately more successful.

> "Make the most of all that comes and the least of all that goes."
> —Sara Teasdale, twentieth century American poet

MAKING ENDS MEET

In addition to having to deal with large doses of stress, many job seekers today are concerned about making ends meet until they find their next job. A good way to combat both problems is to find part-time, temporary, or free-lance work. Working even only a few hours a week will help you stay motivated and upbeat (very important), keep the money rolling in (very, very important), and may very well keep you sane (you decide). As if that's not enough incentive, employers will be impressed with your strong work ethic and sense of initiative. Planning your finances early on can also make a big difference down the road. For more information on this, see chapter 12.

A NOTE TO 50-PLUS JOB SEEKERS

In the current marketplace, many companies are tightening their belts by laying off their higher paid employees, including middle management. Thus, older, more experienced workers are among the hardest hit, with little job security and few other job opportunities. According to a recent article in *Modern Maturity*, statistics show that mature candidates have lengthier job searches (up to twice as long) and typically encounter a variety of stereotypes. Employers may believe that older job seekers lack vitality, are overpaid, or are difficult to train and manage.

To overcome these barriers, the article points out, you should accentuate your strong suits: your maturity, experience, and dependability. You might point out that you don't have caregiving responsibilities that would interfere with your job and you are willing and able to work overtime if necessary. Be sure to emphasize that you are flexible and that your skills are up to date.

The American Association of Retired Persons provides valuable free information for older job seekers and women returning to the job market. For more information, write: AARP, 601 E Street, NW, Washington, DC 20049.

A NOTE TO THE PHYSICALLY CHALLENGED

According to the Americans with Disabilities Act (ADA), employers may not discriminate against job candidates because of their physical handicaps or disabilities. Discrimination is prohibited in job application procedures, hiring, advancement, pay, job training, assignments, benefits, and other privileges of employment. In addition to people with long-term physical impairments, this law protects people with AIDS and those who are HIV-positive, recovering alcoholics, and recovering drug users.

While the ADA prohibits discrimination against job seekers, it does not make the hiring of a physically challenged person mandatory. A disabled job seeker must be able to perform the responsibilities required of that position, and must possess the education, skills, experiences, or licenses required of any other applicant. Furthermore, employers are required to provide reasonable accommodations for you, if your physical impairment requires them.

You should be aware that an employer can not legally ask whether you are physically impaired or question you about the severity of your impairment during a job interview. However, she can ask if you are capable of performing the essential responsibilities of the job. Whether or not you should volunteer information about your disability before you are hired is entirely your choice. However, since employers are only required to accommodate known disabilities, it may be in your best interests to do so.

To make the best impression during an interview, you presentation should be positive and enthusiastic. Emphasize your energy, confidence, motivation, flexibility, and experience. Be sure to explain how well you performed in your past positions.

For more information, contact the Equal Employment Opportunity Commission at 1 (800) 669-EEOC.

IF YOU FEEL YOU'VE BEEN DISCRIMINATED AGAINST . . .

Title VII of the Civil Rights Act forbids employers from discriminating against any person on the basis of sex, age, race, national origin, or religion. Unfortunately, though, discrimination still occurs. If you feel you have been discriminated against, you should contact the Equal Employment Opportunity Commission at 1 (800) 669-EEOC within 180 days of the incident.

The EEOC will investigate and attempt to resolve the charge through conciliation. If it is found that you have in fact been discriminated against, you will be entitled to a remedy which may include hiring, promotion, reinstatement, retroactive pay, and attorney's fees. Contact the EEOC at the above number for more information.

Part IV

The Interview

16
Before the Job Interview

In a typical job search you will have very few interviews relative to the number of companies you contact. Each one is precious!

Even if you are only mildly interested in the company or the position, you should not pass up any opportunity for honing your interviewing skills. Prepare yourself thoroughly and approach each interview with confidence and enthusiasm!

THE SECRET OF INTERVIEW SUCCESS

One of the key messages that you'll want to convey to the interviewer is that you are seriously interested in a career in that particular field at that particular company. If you've been keeping up with industry trends by reading trade publications and talking with industry insiders, you've already won half the battle. But, if in addition to this, you impress the interviewer with your knowledge of that company, you will have a great advantage over the competition. This is the secret of interview success.

To find the information you need, you will need to dig into every resource you can find. You can locate some information in business directories available at libraries. For larger companies you can call the investor relations department and request an annual report and search at the library for recent articles written about the company. Go through the back issues of the industry's trade magazines and look for recent relevant articles. Also, call the firm itself and request more information. Most companies have a brochure or catalog of their products or services. If the firm has a human resources department, ask if they have a recruitment package or any other information that they can send to job seekers.

COLLECTING REFERENCES

At some point before you start interviewing, you will need to prepare a list of three to five references. At least two of these should be professional references, such as from previous employers or close business associates. You can also get valuable references from teachers, professors, volunteer committee heads, and friends who are well-respected in the business arena. However, you should not list family members as references.

Be sure to ask people for their permission before you cite them as references. If they agree, take down their exact job title, the name of the company where they work, and their work address and phone number. You will need to include all of this information on the list you present at job interviews. Do not make the mistake of listing your references on your resume, as it is commonly seen as inappropriate and unprofessional.

Don't forget to send each of your references a thank-you note when your job search is over. Proper etiquette aside, it will help keep your contacts current. You never know when you might need their help again sometime down the road.

LETTERS OF RECOMMENDATION

It can also be helpful to have two or three letters of recommendation on hand to present at each job interview. Like your references, these should be written by past employers and others who are well-respected in business circles. When requesting a written recommendation, you should ask that the letter be sent directly to you (not to an employer) so you can make multiple copies and screen out any references that are less than glowing. Remember also to send a thank-you note promptly to anyone who writes a letter of recommendation for you.

DRESSING FOR SUCCESS

How important is proper dress for a job interview? Well, the final selection of a job candidate will rarely be determined by dress. However, first-round candidates for an opening are often quickly eliminated by inappropriate dress. This is not to say you should go out and invest in a new wardrobe, just be sure that you are able to put together an adequate interview outfit.

Generally, a professional-looking dress or suit with low-heeled shoes makes the best impression. In more conservative industries like law and banking, a suit is a safer bet than a dress. At the same time, some hiring managers in "creative" industries like advertising and publishing look for a more informal, stylish look that reflects the applicant's individuality. Use your best judgement and wear whatever is both professional and comfortable for you.

Top personal grooming is more important than finding the perfect outfit. Be sure that your clothes are immaculately clean and well-fitting, that your hair style is neat and businesslike, and that your shoes are clean and attractive. Avoid excessive jewelry, makeup, or perfume.

Be sure to bring a watch, pen, and pad of paper for taking notes. A briefcase or portfolio, if you have one, will help complete the look of professionalism. Avoid carrying purse if you can—it may detract from your professional image. And don't forget to take a few extra copies of your resume!

TIMING IS EVERYTHING

Although it may seem hard to believe, many job seekers arrive late for interviews. It's easy enough to do. You might simply take a little unplanned extra time to prepare for your interview or underestimate how long it will take to get to the interview location. Don't let yourself make this fatal mistake!

Allow plenty of time to get ready and travel to your job interview. You should not arrive at the interviewer's office more than 10 minutes in advance. However, if you are driving across town, planning 10 minutes of extra time is probably not enough. Try to get to the location at least 30 minutes early; you can then spend 20 minutes in a nearby coffee shop or take a walk around the building. Interviews are important enough to build in a little extra time. Here's another tip: If you have never been to the interview location before, visit it the day before so you know exactly how to get there, access the building, and locate adequate parking.

HAVE THE OBVIOUS ANSWERS READY

You can never be sure exactly what you will be asked at a job interview, but certain questions are more likely to arise than others, and you should be prepared for them. By developing solid answers to questions that are likely to be asked, you will probably be in a better position to answer questions that you hadn't anticipated.

Take a look at your resume, pretending for a moment that you are an employer looking at it for the first time. What questions would you ask? You should bear in mind that questions you are asked in one interview are likely to be repeated in another. Immediately after each interview, take a moment to write down each new question that you were asked; prepare solid responses in case you are asked the questions again.

Some common questions will be relatively easy to prepare for. A recruiter is very likely to ask you for more information about your work history, academic achievements, and personal interests. Be prepared to talk about any one of them for about three minutes.

Try to structure your responses in a way that conveys that you are someone the employer would want to hire. In other words, project yourself as someone who is likely to stay with the company for a number of years, who is achievement oriented, who will fit in well with the other people, who is likeable. Of course, you should also try to present yourself as someone who is capable of doing the job extremely well.

> "A few [job candidates] do well in interviews while others leave in tears. We get nervous, create obstacles, and allow ourselves to fall prey to hungry interviewers. Nervousness is normal, but it's intensified when we do not prepare."
>
> —Toni Blackman, speech team coach
> Howard University

BE PREPARED TO ASK QUESTIONS

Toward the end of the interview the employer will usually ask if you have any questions. You should be prepared to ask one or two questions; if you don't, the employer may think you are ill-prepared or not interested in the company. Use this opportunity to ask questions that subtly demonstrate your knowledge of the firm and the industry, and to underscore your interest in seeking a long-term career position at that company. At the same time, you should not allow your questions to become an interrogation. Two or three thoughtful questions are usually sufficient.

What questions should you ask? Here are some examples:

"What is the next position or positions that this job typically leads to?"

"Assuming I was hired and performed well as a (the position you are applying for) for a number of years, what possible opportunities might this lead to?"

These questions imply that you are an achievement-oriented individual looking for a company where you can build a long-term career.

"I have noticed in the trade press that your firm has a terrific reputation in market-ing. What are the major insights into the marketing process that I might gain from this position?"

"I understand that your company is the market leader in industrial drill bits in North America. I am curious to know how much of the product line is sold over-seas—and whether there are many career opportunities in marketing abroad."

These questions imply that you are very interested in a long-term career in this indus-try and that you might lean toward taking a career with this firm because of its solid repu-tation. Your well-timed and appropriate questions are sure to impress even the toughest interviewer.

"What skills are considered most useful for success in the job I am applying for?"

This question implies you really care about your success at your first job and also pro-vides important information for further interviews—or your follow-up after this interview.

"I would really like to work for your firm. I think it's a great company and I am con-fident I could do this job well. What is the next step of the selection process?"

More than a question, this is a powerful statement that will quickly set you apart from other job hunters. However, you should only make this statement if you mean it. If you are offered the position but then say you need two weeks to think it over, you will lose your credibility. However, even after making this statement, it is reasonable to ask for 24 or 48 hours to "digest the details."

Be sure to save your questions about salary, benefits, and related issues for later, after you receive an offer. You will still be free to negotiate—or to decline the position—at that point. Also, avoid asking any questions that will be difficult or awkward for the recruiter to answer. This is not the time to ask, for example, "Does your company use recycled paper for all of its advertising brochures?"

PRACTICE INTERVIEWING

Once you have developed solid responses to likely interview questions, you should write the questions on index cards. Shuffle the cards and practice answering them into a tape re-corder, moving from one question to the next. Play it back. How did you do? How can you improve? Practice with some friends; ask them for feedback. Then be sure to have your friends ask you many questions you haven't prepared answers to. Are you able to formulate answers quickly? If not, keep practicing.

OVERCOMING NERVOUSNESS

As if formulating solid answers to interview questions isn't tough enough, if you are like most job hunters, you'll have to overcome your own nervousness. Most employers will not condemn job candidates for a bit of nervous behavior—after all, it's only normal—but they will pay close attention to how you hold up under pressure. Displaying excessive nervous-ness can easily eliminate your from further consideration.

One good way to overcome nervousness is to exercise positive thinking. If you're feeling nervous about an upcoming interview, rehearse the scenario in your mind. Think of what you'll say, the questions you'll be asked, and how you'll answer them. Imagine yourself responding calmly, effectively, and in a controlled manner. This type of mental rehearsing won't guarantee your success, but it should help you feel more optimistic and self-confident, which will in fact influence your final presentation in a positive way.

Also, you should practice interviewing as much as you can—especially with real companies. You will become more confident and your answers will become more polished with each interview you have. If you have a terrible interview, don't let it shake your confidence! Realize that everyone has a bad interview experience sooner or later. Learn from it, work on your performance, and keep looking for other opportunities.

COPING WITH A SHY PERSONALITY

For most employers, shyness is not a major problem unless it interferes with your work. In fact, employees are often valued for their shyness because they tend to get along well with other workers and don't participate in office politics. However, shyness can hurt your chances of landing a job if you resist contacting new people or fail to communicate that you're qualified for the position.

There are several steps you can take to overcome shyness. First, when networking, contact only people you feel comfortable with and ask them to introduce you to others. This way, you don't have to call any strangers and you know that all of your inquiries will be welcomed. Begin with friends, relatives, neighbors, and close business associates and you will soon be well on your way to making important contacts.

Another idea that can be particularly valuable for first-time job seekers is to seek out volunteer work or an internship in your chosen field. Volunteering and interning allow you the opportunity to show an employer your skills and abilities rather than having to discuss them in a pressure-filled interview. Many employers prefer to hire volunteers and interns because they are already familiar with their strengths and work habits.

You probably won't be able to avoid job interviews altogether, though. Your best bet is to manage your shyness as best you can. For the first few minutes of your interview, just listen to the interviewer talk, interject a few questions or comments here and there, and let yourself relax. When you're asked about your accomplishments, simply be frank and relate what occurred. Don't feel pressured into giving the "hard sell" by telling the recruiter that you were brilliant or that you did a great job if you are uncomfortable doing so. Let recruiters come to their own conclusions; they'll not only see the positive qualities that led to your accomplishments, but they'll appreciate your frank but unassuming manner as well.

If it makes you feel more comfortable, tell the recruiter right away that you tend to be shy and you're feeling a little nervous. This often breaks the ice and will keep the employer from concluding that you're trying to hide something or that your shyness is a sign of some larger problem.

INTERVIEW STRATEGY

For your first few interviews, or at least until you are feeling very comfortable, focus your efforts on remaining calm and collected. Listen carefully to what the recruiter is saying and respond promptly and thoroughly to the recruiter's questions. Don't try too hard. If you have been practicing your responses, you should be able to offer appropriate answers without too much difficulty.

Once you begin to feel more confident about interviewing you may wish to think strategically about each interview. One effective tactic is to adjust your speed of speech to match that of the interviewer. People tend to talk at the speed at which they like to be spoken to. If you can adjust your speech rate to that of the recruiter without sounding unnatural, the recruiter will probably feel more comfortable (after all, interviewing others isn't much fun, either) and have a more favorable impression of you.

> "Don't get stuck in the interview zone by letting it get you down. Remember the five P's: Proper Preparation Prevents Poor Performance. Preparation also helps you to feel good when you walk in the door. That good feeling stays with you when you walk out the door— whether or not you get the job."
>
> —Toni Blackman, speech team coach
> Howard University

Another strategy is to adapt your answers to match the type of company for which you are interviewing. For example, if you are interviewing for a job at a large product marketing company that emphasizes group decision-making and spends much of its energy focused on battles for market share with its competitors, you might want to talk about how much you enjoy team sports—especially being part of a team and competing to win.

When filling professional career positions, few companies will make a job offer after only one interview. Usually, the purpose of the first interview is to narrow down the field of applicants to a small number of very promising candidates. During the first meeting, then, the ideal strategy is to stand out from a large field of competitors in a positive way. The best way to do this is to subtly emphasize one of your key, distinctive strengths as much as possible throughout the interview.

During later interviews, the competition for the position will drop off and recruiters will tend to look not for strengths, but for weaknesses. At this point you should focus on presenting yourself as a well-balanced choice for the position. You will want to listen carefully to the interviewer's questions so you can determine her underlying concerns and try to dispel them.

Every Woman's Essential Job Hunting & Resume Book

17
At the Interview

You've scheduled an interview.

By now, you have probably spent a great deal of time preparing yourself for this. However, you must not let your practice and preparation become a disadvantage. Once the interview begins, your focus must be on interacting well with the interviewer—as opposed to trying to recall the exact responses you prepared earlier. If you prepared for the interview well, your conduct and responses will convey to the interviewer the image that you want to project without effort.

THOSE CRUCIAL FIRST FEW MOMENTS

The first minutes of the interview are the most important. A recruiter begins sizing up your potential the instant you walk in the room. If you make a bad impression initially, the recruiter may rule you out immediately and not pay close attention to your performance during the rest of the interview. An excellent initial impression, on the other hand, will put a favorable glow on everything else you say during the rest of the interview—and could well encourage the recruiter to ask less demanding questions.

How can you ensure that you make a terrific first impression? The easiest answer is to be sure you are dressed well. When the recruiter meets you, your clothes and grooming will be noticed first. As mentioned earlier, nothing less than impeccable grooming is acceptable. Your attire must be professional and squeaky clean.

In virtually the same instant the recruiter notices your appearance, even before either of you speaks, your body language will begin to affect the way you are perceived. Even an inexperienced recruiter who is not consciously seeking to make a "first read" will notice and react to your body language. Here are some important things to think about:

- Are you smiling before being greeted? Smiling sincerely is a universally attractive trait.
- Do you approach the recruiter with a confident, self-assured gait or do you slump your shoulders and look at the floor?

- Do you extend your right hand naturally to begin a firm (but not viselike) handshake?
- Are your briefcase, note pad, and coat in your left hand or do you have to juggle them around in order to shake hands?
- Do you make just enough eye contact without staring at the recruiter?
- Do your eyes travel naturally to and from the recruiter's face as you begin to talk?
- Do you remember the recruiter's name and pronounce it with confidence?
- Do you wait for the recruiter to invite you to sit down before doing so?
- Alternatively, if the recruiter forgets to invite you to take a seat, do you awkwardly ask if you may be seated as though to remind the recruiter of a lapse in etiquette? Or do you gracefully help yourself to a seat?
- Do you make small talk easily, or do you act formal and reserved, as though under attack?

As you can see, much of the first impression you make at an interview will be dramatically affected by how relaxed and confident you feel. This is why it is so important to practice for each interview—so you can truly give your best impression.

> "Anyone who's ever taken a sales course knows potential buyers are more interested in how you can benefit them than in how your product or service works. While discussing your experience is useful, it isn't nearly as intriguing as demonstrating how your background and skills can help the company or department improve productivity or solve a particular problem."
>
> —Taunee Besson, President
> Career Dimensions

STRUCTURED OR UNSTRUCTURED?

Interviewing styles generally fall into one of two categories, structured or unstructured. In a structured interview, the recruiter asks a prescribed set of questions, seeking relatively brief answers. In the unstructured interview, the recruiter asks more open-ended questions to prod you to give longer responses and reveal as much as possible about yourself, your background, and your aspirations. Some recruiters will mix both styles, typically beginning with more objective questions and asking more open-ended questions as the interview progresses.

Be very careful to answer questions in the manner the recruiter desires. Try to determine as soon as possible if the recruiter is conducting a structured or unstructured interview; respond to the questions accordingly. As you answer the questions, watch for signals from the recruiter as to whether to your responses are too short or too long. For example, if the recruiter is nodding or looking away, wrap up your answer as quickly as possible.

Following the style the recruiter establishes will make the interview easier and more comfortable and will leave the recruiter with a more favorable impression of you.

LOOK ON THE BRIGHT SIDE!

Many job candidates kill their chances for a job by making negative comments during an interview. Never make a negative statement about a former boss or colleague—even if it is completely true and fully justified. If the recruiter asks why you were fired from your last job, do not say "My boss was unfair" or "I didn't get along with my co-workers." A recruiter would rather hire someone who was fired than someone who either doesn't get along with people or shifts blame to others.

On the other hand, you can greatly increase your chances of getting any job by projecting a positive, upbeat attitude during your interview. This is one of the very best ways you can stand out from the competition. You can project this image by smiling from time to time during the interview; by responding to interview questions with enthusiasm; by demonstrating excitement about your past accomplishments; and by showing optimism about the prospect of starting or continuing your career.

> "From an employer's point of view an attractive candidate is one who thinks and talks about opportunities and success, not limitations and failures."
>
> —Bruce Bloom, author
> *Fast Track to the Best Job*

HANDLING IMPOSSIBLE QUESTIONS

One of the biggest fears that job candidates harbor about interviews is the unknown question for which they have no answer. To make matters worse, some recruiters may ask a question knowing full well that you can't possibly answer it!

Sometimes recruiters do ask seemingly impossible questions, not because they enjoy seeing you squirm in your seat; rather, they want to judge how you might respond to pressure or tension on the job. If you are asked a tough question that you simply can't answer, think about it for a few seconds. Then with a confident smile and without apology, simply say, "I can't answer that question."

ANSWERING QUESTIONS ABOUT YOUR SALARY HISTORY

By all means, if you are asked about your salary history, do not embellish. More and more companies are starting to verify applicants' pay history, some even demanding to see W-2 income forms from job seekers. Even if you get the job, a falsehood discovered even years later is grounds for immediate dismissal. Don't leave yourself open to this kind of trouble.

ANSWERING QUESTIONS THAT REQUIRE COMMITMENT

You may, even in some first interviews, be asked questions that seem to elicit a tremendous commitment on your behalf. For example, the recruiter might ask, "Would you be willing to move across the country to our technical training center for two years?" or "Would you be willing to work 12-hour shifts on Saturdays and Sundays?"

While it may be true that such questions are extremely unfair to ask during an initial job interview, you may have nothing to gain and everything to lose by saying no—or even, "I need to think about it." If you are asked such a question unexpectedly during an initial job interview, you can simply say, "That's certainly a possibility" or "I'm willing to consider that."

Later, if you receive an offer, you can find out what specific work conditions apply and then decide if you wish to accept the position. You might explain to the recruiter that now that you have had time to think about it, you cannot accept a position that involves (for instance) relocation, but you would like to be considered for other positions that may open up in the future.

ILLEGAL INTERVIEW QUESTIONS

Illegal interview questions probe into your private life or personal background. Federal law forbids employers from discriminating against any person on the basis of sex, age, race, national origin, or religion. For instance, an interviewer may not ask you about your age or your date of birth. *However*, she may ask you if you are over 18 years of age.

If you are asked an illegal question at a job interview, keep in mind that many employers simply don't know what is legal and illegal. One strategy is to try to discern the concerns behind the question and then address them. For instance, if the employer asks you about your plans to have children, she may be concerned that you won't be able to fulfill the travel requirements of the position. Sexist? You bet. But it's to your advantage to try to alleviate her concerns.

"With illegal questions, your response must be positive—that's the only way you're going to get the job offer, and getting a job offer allows you to leverage other jobs. You don't have to work for a discriminatory company, but you can certainly use the firm to get something better."

—Martin Yate, author
Knock 'em Dead: The Ultimate Job Seeker's Handbook

Try to draw out the real issue behind the question by saying something like, "I'm not quite sure I understand what you're getting at. Would you please explain to me how this issue is relevant to the position?" Once her concerns are on the table, you can reassure the employer by saying something like, "I'm very interested in developing my career. Travel is definitely not a problem for me—in fact, I enjoy it tremendously. Now, let me direct your attention to my experience and expertise in . . ."

Alternatively, you may choose to answer the question or gracefully point out that the question is illegal and decline to respond. Avoid reacting in a hostile fashion—remember that you can always decide later to decline the job offer.

Any of the following responses are acceptable ways to handle these tricky situations without blowing your chances for a job offer. Choose the response that is most comfortable for you.

"What religion do you practice?"

Answer #1:   "I make it a point not to mix my personal beliefs with my work, if that's what you mean. I assure you that I value my career too much for that."

Answer #2:   "I'm not quite sure I understand what you're getting at. Would you please explain to me how this issue is relevant to the position?"

Answer #3: "That question makes me uncomfortable. I'd really rather not answer it."

"How old are you?"

Answer #1: "I am in my fifties and have over 30 years of experience in this industry. My area of expertise is in . . ."

Answer #2: "I'm too young to retire but I'm old enough to know better than to answer a question like that."

Answer #3: "I'm not quite sure I understand what you're getting at. Would you please explain to me how this issue is relevant to the position?"

Answer #4: "That question makes me uncomfortable. I'd really rather not answer it."

"Are you married?"

Answer #1: "No."

Answer #2: "Yes, I am. But I keep my family life separate from my work life so that I can put all my effort into my job. I am flexible when it comes to travel and late hours, as my references can confirm."

Answer #3: "I'm not quite sure I understand what you're getting at. Would you please explain to me how this issue is relevant to the position?"

Answer #4: "That question makes me uncomfortable. I'd really rather not answer it."

"Do you have children?"

Answer #1: "No."

Answer #2: "Yes, I do. But I keep my family life separate from my work life so that I can put all my effort into my job. I am flexible when it comes to travel and late hours, as my references can confirm."

Answer #3: "I'm not quite sure I understand what you're getting at. Would you please explain to me how this issue is relevant to the position?"

Answer #4: "That question makes me uncomfortable. I'd really rather not answer it."

"Do you plan to have children?"

Answer #1: "No."

Answer #2: "It's certainly a consideration, but if I do, it won't be for some time. I want to do the best job I can for this company and have no plans to leave just as I begin to make meaningful contributions."

Answer #3:   "I can't answer that right now. But if I ever do decide to have children, I would not let it detract from my work. Becoming a parent is important, but my career is certainly very important to me too. I plan on putting all of my efforts into this job and this company."

Answer #4:   "I'm not quite sure I understand what you're getting at. Would you please explain to me how this issue is relevant to the position?"

Answer #5:   "That question makes me uncomfortable. I'd really rather not answer it."

18

Commonly Asked Interview Questions— and Their Answers

Answering a battery of interview questions can feel something like running a gauntlet. A little preparation, though, can help see you through safe and sound.

The interview questions and answers listed in this chapter should give you a sense of how questions should be handled. They should not be used as the basis of "canned" or scripted answers. Adapt these responses to your own circumstances, and remember that the way you respond can be just as important as what you actually say. Be positive, smile, and make eye contact with the interviewer and above all else, go with the flow!

GENERAL QUESTIONS

"Tell me about a time when your employer was not happy with your job performance."

"It was my first week on the job as a paralegal. There were two letters that had typos in them. Frankly, I had been a little sloppy with them. But that's all that comes to mind. Ms. Heilman did tell me regularly that she was very happy with my work."

"Have you ever been fired?"

"Yes. I had a part-time courier job during college. I became violently ill with a stomach bug after lunch one day and had to call in sick 30 minutes before my shift began. I was immediately told that I was fired. I knew it was difficult for my boss to get a substitute courier on such short notice. But I was very dizzy and thought there would be too much risk of an accident if I reported to work."

"Who is the toughest employer you have ever had and why?"

"That would be Ms. Henson at Franklin Associates. She would push people to their limits when it got busy, and she was a stickler for detail. But she was always fair, and she rewarded good, hard work. I would call her a tough boss, but a good boss."

"Have you ever had to work with a manager who was unfair to you, or who was just plain hard to talk to?"

"Actually, I've never run into that. Of course, my current boss has to work under time constraints—just like everyone else—and she sometimes has to phrase things succinctly if our department is going to meet its goals. But I've never considered that unfair or hard to handle. It's just part of the job. My supervisors and I have always gotten along quite well."

> Never, under any circumstances, criticize a current or former employer, no matter how many times the interviewer gives you the opportunity to do so. What the interviewer is trying to find out here is not whether you've worked for difficult people before, but rather, whether you will bad-mouth them.

"Why do you want to work in retailing?"

"I have been fascinated by the retail trade for as long as I can remember. To me each store is a stage or theater for its merchandise; there is an infinite variety of ways in which the exact same merchandise can be sold. I know it's a very challenging field, too. Merchants need to think about the current fashion trends, the needs of local consumers, building a niche in the marketplace, and all the other aspects of running a business. Also, retail is a field that is changing very quickly today, and I want to see firsthand the direction retailing is taking."

"What other firms are you interviewing at and for what positions?"

"Actually, I have definitely decided to pursue a career as a restaurant manager, so I am only applying for restaurant management training programs. I have recently had interviews with several other large national fast-food chains such as Super Burger and Clackey's Chicken."

> Often, the candidate tries to impress the employer by naming some large firms in unrelated industries with completely different types of jobs. This is a big mistake! What employers want to hear is that you are interviewing for similar jobs in the same industry at similar firms (such as their competitors). This illustrates that you are commited to finding a job in your field of interest and are likely to be a low-risk hire.

"Have you thought about why you might prefer to work with our firm as opposed to one of the other firms to which you've applied?"

"Yes. I like your policy of promotion from within. I think the company's growth record is impressive and I am sure it will continue. Your firm's reputation for superior marketing is particularly important to me because, of course, that is my field of interest. Most important of all, it seems that your firm would offer me a lot of opportunities—not just for possible advancement but also to learn about many different product lines—all within one company."

"What are your salary requirements?"

"I would expect a salary that is comparable to the going rate for someone in my field with my skills and expertise. Salary, however, is not my only consideration. I'm most interested in this opportunity because I think it represents a good match between what you're looking for and my qualifications. What kind of figure do you have in mind?"

"Which do you prefer—working alone or with others?"

"My own experience has been that I'm comfortable with a combination of both. When there's something on my desk that has to be done well within a certain period of time, I'm always excited by the challenge of that, and I find I don't need much support once I understand the basics of the task before me. However, in every organization, there are times when teamwork is required, and I find that it can also be very rewarding to help attain a departmental or company goal."

"Where would you like to be in five years?"

"I plan to remain in the banking industry for the foreseeable future. I hope that within five years I will have developed a successful track record as a loan officer, first perhaps with consumer loans, but with business loans. Ideally, I would hope that within five years I will also have advanced to servicing middle-market-size companies."

"Do you plan to attend graduate school?"

"Definitely not on a full-time basis. At some point, though, I might like to take some courses at night that could contribute to my work performance."

> A fatal error many job seekers make is telling an employer that they intend to further pursue their education. Though this is an honorable intention, employers are interested in candidates who are ready to begin a career and are likely to commit to that company for a number of years.

"Would you be willing to relocate to another city?"

"I would prefer to be based here, but it is certainly a possibility I'd be willing to consider."

"Tell me about yourself."

"I have a tremendous amount of energy and love to be challenged. I set up a goal for myself to have the highest pace of anyone in the office without neglecting the quality of my work. I also enjoy being around other people, working with them, and doing anything I can to help my co-workers. For example, I really enjoyed my position as a customer service manager at Jessup Products, Inc. I felt continually challenged by solving customer concerns and problems and felt as if I was really making a positive contribution to the company."

"What would you do if I told you that I thought you were giving a very poor interview today?"

"Well, the first thing I'd do would be to ask you if there was any specific part of the interview process that you thought I might have mishandled. After that, I'd think back and try to remember if there had been any faulty communication on my part. Then I'd try to review any possible problems I had understanding your questions, and I'd ask for clarification if I needed it. Finally, if we had time, I'd try to respond more fully and appropriately to the problem areas you identified for me."

> Interviewers like to ask "stress questions" like these to see how well you hold up under pressure. Your best bet is to stay calm, relaxed, and don't allow your confidence to be shaken.

"How would you respond to a defaulted form Z-65 counterderivative renewal request if your manager ordered you to do so, and if the policy under which the executive board resolves such issues were currently under review?"

Sometimes recruiters ask seemingly impossible questions, just to see how you will respond. They usually don't ask such questions because want to see you squirm in your seat; rather, they want to judge how you might respond to pressure or tension on the job. No matter how it may feel at the time, being subjected to a ridiculous question such as this one is probably a very good sign. If you are asked a tough question that you simply can't answer, think about it for a few seconds. Then with a confident smile and without apology, simply say something like, "I don't know, but if you hire me, I'll sure find out for you."

QUESTIONS FOR STUDENTS AND RECENT GRADS

"Are you satisfied with the grades you received in school?"

"School was a wonderful experience for me. I really enjoyed learning new ideas, I studied consistently, and I was attentive in class. But I never believed in cramming before the night of an exam just to get a higher grade or staying up all night finishing a term paper. I really believe I learned just as much as many students who 'went for the grades.'"

"Why did you decide to major in history?"

"It was a difficult choice because I was also attracted to government, international relations, and economics. But the study of history allowed me to combine all three, especially since I focused on economic history. What's more, I found several of the professors in the department to be exceptionally knowledgeable and stimulating."

"Was there a course that you found particularly challenging?"

"Initially I was completely overwhelmed by the introductory chemistry course that I took last year. No matter how hard I studied, I seemed to be getting nowhere. I failed the first three quizzes. So I tried a new approach. Instead of just studying by myself, I had a friend who is chemistry major help me with my studies. I also began to seek help from the professor after class. And I found that more time spent in the lab was critical. I ended up with a B+ in the course and felt I achieved a solid understanding of the material. More than that, I learned that tackling a new field of study sometimes require a new approach, not just hard work, and that the help of others can be crucial!"

"Why didn't you participate more in extracurricular activities?"

"I wanted to give as much effort as possible to my studies. I came from a high school in a very small town where I received a lot of A's but this did not prepare me very well for college. So I have studied very hard. I have, however, found time to explore the city, make new friends, and I do socialize informally on weekends."

QUESTIONS FOR AT-HOME MOMS AND HOMEMAKERS ENTERING THE JOB MARKET FOR THE FIRST TIME

"I see that you do not have very much past work experience. What qualities do you have that especially qualify you for this position?"

"The bookkeeping position you advertised calls for a thorough knowledge of accounting skills; I have managed my husband's and my personal accounts diligently and accurately for the past 18 years. I also instituted a budget plan for our whole family to follow which enabled us to save over $30,000 in just four years. As for organizational skills, I organized a car pool for our daughter's little league team which, if you have children, you know is no easy feat. Also, the fact that you are a plant nursery intrigues me because I am an avid gardener. It seems as if my skills and interests fit your needs perfectly."

"I see that you do not have very much past work experience. What qualities do you have that especially qualify you for this position?"

"Although I do not have a great deal of formal job experience, I gained valuable skills working with my husband to establish and grow a small furniture store. I handled all the billing and receiving, essentially was the customer service department, decorated the store, implemented our first computer system, and eventually began consulting on interior design issues with customers. Although I only worked there part-time and was not paid, my contributions were substantial. I feel that the skills I've learned from this experience, my knowledge of the furniture industry, and my talent for design make me an excellent candidate for this position."

"Why are you interested in the public relations industry?"

"Several years ago, a close family friend ran for a seat on the local school board. Since my children were all grown by this time and I had no formal job to speak of, I was able to devote much of my time to her campaign. I found myself exhilarated by the work and I learned a great deal about campaigning, in which public relations, of course, plays a key role. The elections are long since over, but I found that my interest in pubic relations has not subsided. I've read just about everything on the subject that I can find and I've talked with several people who work in the field. The more I learn, the more fascinated I become. I'm convinced that I have the talent, creativity, and energy to make it in PR. I'd like have the opportunity to prove it to you."

QUESTIONS FOR AT-HOME MOMS RETURNING TO THE JOB MARKET

"Your resume does not list any job experience in the past few years. Why not?"

"I took five years off to raise my son, Jason, who is now in kindergarten. It was a difficult decision for me but, at the time, I felt I would not be able to commit myself 100 percent to my career with such tremendous responsibilities at home. And I didn't feel it would be fair to my employer to give any less than my complete and total commitment. I feel it was the right decision for me at the time, but now I feel refreshed and ready to devote myself full-time to my career."

"Your resume indicates that you have been working for the past two years as a part-time clerk at Reliable Insurance Brokers. How will this experience help you in your career in banking?"

"The company was in the process of computerizing its files. The primary task for which I was hired was to check the computerized files for accuracy vis-a-vis the manual files. I recorded premium payments, prepared bank deposits, and sorted payables. Not only did this help me keep my accounting skills current, I also learned valuable computer skills that will certainly help me become even more efficient and productive in my next position in banking."

QUESTIONS FOR CAREER CHANGERS

"Why do you want to leave your current position?"

"I've learned quite a bit about the plastics industry from my current position and am very glad to have had the opportunities I have at Fiske, Inc. However, I've found that my interests really lie in research and development, which Fiske has recently decided to phase out over the next two years. And that is why I am so interested in this organization, because, as I understand, Randy Corporation places a great deal of emphasis on R&D, as well as being a respected leader in the industry."

"Why would you want to leave an established career at an employment agency for an essentially entry-level position in marketing?"

"I've enjoyed my work at the agency and have gained many valuable skills from it. At the same time, however, I feel as if I've stopped growing. I no longer feel challenged by my work. I've thought about this for a long time and I feel confident that it's time for a change.

"As for my interest in marketing, last year my teenage children and some of the other neighborhood kids decided to design and sell tee shirts to benefit a local family who lost their home to a fire. I pitched in by designing and posting posters, placing advertisements in local newspapers, and selling shirts outside grocery stores and shopping malls. At first, I really didn't give it a lot of thought, but when I saw the fruits of my labor, I began to get very excited about it. I learned that you can have a great product and a great cause, but if nobody knows about it, you're dead in the water. I finally felt like I was making a difference—and I was good at it, too. Since then, I've taken two introductory marketing courses and am planning to enroll in a part-time degree program this fall.

"Furthermore, I will be able to use many of the skills and abilities I've gained at the employment agency in the marketing field. After all, working for an employment agency *is* marketing—marketing the agency to corporate clients and job seekers, and marketing job seekers to corporate clients."

"How much notice would you have to give your current employer if I offered you this position?"

"I would feel obliged to offer my current employer two weeks notice. But if my boss does not object, I may be able to leave earlier."

19
After the Interview

You've made it through the toughest part, but now what? First, breathe a sigh of relief! Then, as soon as you've left the interview site, write down your thoughts about the interview while they're still fresh in your mind. Ask yourself these key questions:

- *What does the position entail?*
- *What do you like and dislike about the position and the company?*
- *Did you make any mistakes or have trouble answering any of the questions?*
- *Did you feel you were well prepared?*
- *If not, what could you do to improve your performance in the future?*

Carefully consider all of these questions; if you find that your performance was lacking, work to improve it.

Be sure to record the name and title of the person you interviewed with, as well as the names and titles of anyone else you may have met. Ideally, you will have collected their business cards. Don't forget to write down what the next agreed-upon step would be. Will the recruiter contact you? How soon?

WRITING YOUR FOLLOW-UP LETTER

Next, write a brief follow-up letter thanking the interviewer. You should do this immediately—within 24 hours of the interview, if possible—in order to make sure that you stay in the forefront of the recruiter's mind. Be sure to:

- Express your appreciation for the opportunity to interview with the recruiter.
- Express your continued enthusiasm about the position and the company.
- Recap your strengths, being careful to relate them to the requirements of the job and the company.
- Request to meet again.

The letter should be typewritten and no longer than one page. Make sure that the letter is personalized—don't send out a form letter!

(See the end of this chapter for an example of a follow-up letter.)

WHEN TO CALL

Allow the employer 5 to 10 days to contact you after receiving your letter. If you still haven't heard anything after this time, you should follow up with a phone call. Express your continued interest in the firm and in the position; inquire as to whether or not any decisions have been made or when you will be notified.

WHAT'S NEXT?

Don't be discouraged if you do not get an immediate response from an employer—most companies interview many applicants before making a final decision. The key is to remain fresh in the recruiter's mind. Beyond that, it's a waiting game.

Take advantage of this time to contact other firms and schedule more interviews. This way, if a rejection does come, you have other options open. Continuing to actively job hunt and interview is a good idea even if you end up receiving a job offer. Ultimately, you'll have a number of opportunities to choose from and you'll be in a better position to negotiate terms.

If you place too much importance on a single interview, not only are you bound to be much more disappointed if the offer doesn't come through, you will be wasting valuable time and energy. So keep plugging!

HANDLING REJECTION

Rejection is inevitable, and it will happen to you as it happens to all other job hunters. The key is to be prepared for it and not take it personally.

> "Failure is an event, not a person."
>
> —Zig Ziglar, author
> *Zig Ziglar's Secrets of Closing the Sale*

One way you can turn rejection around is by contacting each person who sends you a rejection letter. Thank your contact for considering you for the position and request that she keep you in mind for future openings. If you feel comfortable, you may want to ask her for suggestions to help you improve your chances of getting a job in that industry or for the names of people who might be looking for someone with your skills. Ask, "What would you do in my situation? Who would you call?"

Two cautions are in order. First, do not ask employers to tell you why they didn't hire you. Not only will this put the employer in a very awkward position, you will probably get a very negative reaction. And second, realize that even if you contact employers solely for impartial feedback, not everyone will be willing to talk with you.

But, above everything else, don't give up. Stay positive and motivated, and learn from the process. Success could be right around the corner!

Sample Follow-Up Letter

460 Brook Road
Santa Fe, New Mexico 87541
(505) 555-5555

September 22, 1995

Pat Cummings
Director of Human Resources
Any Corporation
1140 Main Street
Chicago, IL 60605

Dear Ms. Cummings:

Thank you for the opportunity to discuss your opening for a statistician. I enjoyed meeting with you and Mr. Tate and learning more about Any Corporation.

I believe that my experience at the Department of Labor and my educational background in statistics, economics, and business administration qualify me for the position. My extensive knowledge of computers and statistical software would also be especially valuable to me as a statistician with your firm.

I was particularly impressed with Any Corporation's strong commitment to innovation and growth, as well as its plans to expand into the overseas market. I feel that this type of environment would challenge me to do my best work.

I would like to meet with you again to further discuss this position. If I do not hear from you within the next five days, I will call you to schedule a time that is convenient for us both. In the meantime, I will be happy to provide any other information you may need to assist in your decision.

Sincerely,

Joan Smith

Joan Smith

Part V

Career Planning

20
The Job Offer

Congratulations! You've earned a job offer—or maybe even a few. What do you do now?

Let's start with some basic considerations. What is the minimum salary you can live on? What is the going rate in the current market for your particular position? Don't wait until you get to the offer stage to determine these figures, though. You should know your worth long before entering into negotiations with potential employers.

To consider the offer seriously, you should feel confident that this is a job you really want, the field is one you'd like to pursue a career in, and you are willing to live and work in the area in question. Ask yourself: Is the lifestyle and work schedule associated with the potential new occupation one you would enjoy? Presumably you've had time to think about these issues and now is the time to make final decisions.

IMPORTANT FACTORS TO CONSIDER

Once you've received the offer, of course, you should have all the information about the position necessary for you to make a sound decision. This includes:

- Start date
- Job title and associated responsibilities
- Potential for career progression
- Salary, overtime and compensation
- Bonus structure
- Tuition reimbursement
- Vacation and parental leave policy
- Life, medical, and dental insurance coverage
- Pension plan
- Job location
- Travel requirements

If you're unsure of any of this information, don't assume that it will be to your satisfaction. Contact the personnel representative or recruiting contact and confirm all important details. Ideally these issues would have been covered in a second or third interview.

MONEY

Money may seem like the biggest criterion in accepting a job, but it can often cloud the decision-making process. Don't accept a job that you are not enthusiastic about simply because the starting salary is a few thousand dollars higher. (After taxes, the few thousand dollars may be virtually meaningless.) It's probably more important to find a job that lets you do something you enjoy. Ask yourself whether the job presents a career path with upward movement and long-range income potential.

> "A career is not a sprint, it is a marathon. If you want to make a lot of money, you can get it with a dead-end job. These jobs pay maximum dollar for what you know today but don't teach any skills that will make you marketable tomorrow."
>
> —Martin Yate, author
> *Knock 'em Dead: The Ultimate Job Seeker's Handbook*

BENEFITS

Benefits can make a big difference in your compensation package—don't overlook them! Perhaps the most important benefit to consider is health insurance. With health insurance costs skyrocketing, you should be sure to find out if the company covers these costs in full. If the company, like many others, only pays a percentage of these costs, make certain that you can afford to pay the difference out of your own pocket.

What about life, dental, and disability insurance? Does the company have a bonus structure or profit-sharing plan? This can contribute significantly to your salary. Is there a pension plan? What is the organization's policy on vacation and sick time? You should consider all of these factors carefully.

If you plan to continue your education, it is important for you to find out if the organization will pay for your tuition and if the employer will give you the time to attend classes. Some organizations offer tuition incentives but require so much overtime that it is very difficult to take advantage of the benefit.

CAREER PROGRESSION

Career progression is another important factor in evaluating an offer. Some organizations may bring you on board at a relatively high level and then curtail your movement. Be clear about future opportunities for advancement. Find out how often performance reviews are conducted—this could have a considerable impact on your salary in the long run. Find out how many women are in decision-making positions. This can be a good indication of whether or not a company is progressive in encouraging women to join its upper ranks.

WORK ENVIRONMENT

Another factor to consider is the kind of environment you will be working in. Is the company's atmosphere comfortable, challenging, and exciting? Consider specifics, including office or work station setting, privacy, proximity to coworkers, amount of space, noise level, and lighting. What is the level of interaction among co-workers? Some organizations strongly encourage teamwork and dialogue among staff, while others prefer to emphasize individual accomplishment and discourage a great deal of interaction among employees. Which approach do you prefer?

Most importantly, what is the personality and management style of your potential supervisor? Remember, you don't have to become friends with your boss—or even like her—but you do need to be able to work effectively with her. It's important to consider all of these factors carefully; if you don't like the work environment before you accept the job, you probably won't like it as an employee.

DO YOUR HOMEWORK

Supplement the information provided by the organization by searching journals and newspapers for articles about the company and, if possible, by talking to current employees. Try to get objective comments—not, for instance, information from someone who was recently fired by the company. Alumni of your college or university who hold similar positions or are employed by the same organization may be an excellent source of information.

THE ART OF NEGOTIATION

Now that you have a job offer, you may be thinking that you can sit back and relax. Wrong! One of the most important tasks in your job search is still ahead of you—negotiating terms. If you feel uncomfortable with this prospect, you are not alone. Many job candidates feel uncomfortable discussing money and end up accepting the first salary offer they hear. But negotiating is definitely worth your while. Not only can it result in a better starting salary and benefits, it will also affect later pay raises and future earnings with this and other employers.

But how do you know whether or not an offer is fair? First of all, and most importantly, you need to know your market value. You can do this by contacting trade associations, local employment agencies, and people who work in comparable positions. Keep in mind, though, that salaries often vary according to location, as does the cost of living. An ad executive in Portland, Maine, for example, would not be likely to earn a salary comparable to an ad executive in New York City.

Whenever possible, you should try to get the employer to volunteer salary information first. If the employer indicates the position pays, for example, between $25,000 and $30,000, you should ask for a salary toward the top of that range or even slightly above it. On the other hand, if the employer offers you a specific figure, it's likely that it is at the midpoint of the range established for the position. For example, if the employer says she can't offer you more than $25,000, it often means that $25,000 is the midpoint.

Most times, however, the employer will ask you to volunteer your salary requirements first. In this case, you should be as nonspecific as possible. Instead of an exact amount, state a range and indicate that you are willing to negotiate. Be careful to convey the attitude that the job is more important than the money. You might say something like, "Although money is an important factor, I'm most interested in this opportunity because I think it represents a good match between your needs and my qualifications."

Companies will almost always, if they can, negotiate up to some degree if they feel your requirements are reasonable. Of course, having other job offers puts you in a better negotiating position as does being employed while you're job searching. Studies show time and again that employed job seekers are offered higher salaries than those who are unemployed. At the same time, however, some industries are less open to negotiation than others. The "glamour" fields such as entertainment, advertising, public relations, and publishing are regularly deluged with interested job seekers and therefore do not need to be very flexible about salary.

> "Figuring out which career move is right for you is similar to trying to find a suitable marriage partner. When you try to take a spontaneous approach to either, your chances for success are lessened."
>
> —Taunee Besson, President
> Career Dimensions

Salary, however, is not your only consideration. Benefits can make a big difference in your overall cost of living. If you are disappointed with the benefits package you are offered, find out what is negotiable. Some organizations offer flexible benefits packages or "menu" benefit plans where an employee gets to choose from a variety of options. If it hasn't been discussed previously, now is the best time to ask about such plans.

If you're unable to negotiate an arrangement you feel comfortable with, this may be an indication that you should consider other offers or continue looking for a more suitable position. Don't make the mistake of accepting a position that you are unhappy with. Trust your instincts—if you are dissatisfied with the employer before your start date, this feeling will probably have a negative impact on your work and your success. It's also a feeling that's not likely to go away once you come on board.

At the same time, however, keep in mind that competition for jobs is fierce in today's tough economy. In many instances, employers will not have to look very far to find somebody else to fill a position you turned down. Keep your expectations realistic and don't ask for the stars. Once you've been working for that employer for a while and have proven yourself to be a valuable commodity, you can attempt further negotiations.

MAKING YOUR FINAL DECISION

Probably the most important factor to consider in evaluating an offer is whether you will be happy with the job and accomplish what is important to you. Don't accept a job because your friend works there or because a relative thinks it sounds great. Talk the offer over with other people but trust your own reasoning ability. If you are confused, discuss your concerns with a career counselor and then make an informed decision based on what is right for you.

21
Career Planning

Although job hunting may temporarily bring career planning to the forefront of your priorities, career planning is something you should always be thinking about, regardless of your employment situation. Career planning doesn't just mean making sure your workplace skills are up to date, that you can type 90 WPM, and that you know your way around the latest computer technologies (although these can be important). It means establishing specific goals for the upcoming year and for five, ten, and twenty years down the road. It also means networking continually—not just while you are looking for a new job—and keeping on top of leaders and trends in your industry and your company.

Remember, in these lean and mean times every job is expendable under the right circumstances, regardless of your training and experience. A shift in your industry, or a merger, acquisition, or reorganization can eliminate your role overnight. That's why career planning is so important.

USE THIS TIME TO UPDATE YOUR SKILLS

If you are out of work while you are job hunting, use this valuable time to update your skills. Take a local computer course, enroll in a part-time degree program, read up on the latest business and trade literature, attend a seminar. Not only will this present you with some terrific networking opportunities, it will improve your marketability.

> "People of accomplishment rarely sit back and let things happen to them. They go out and happen to *things*."
> —Elinor Smith, twentieth century novelist

KEEP YOUR NETWORKING CONTACTS ALIVE

As you've probably realized by now, it's important to keep networking even after you've found a job. Joining a professional association is a great way to do this. See chapter 14 for more information about some organizations you may be interested in. For information about associations that specialize in your field or industry, check your local library for the *Encyclopedia of Associations* or *National Trade and Professional Associations of the United States.*

By all means, once you've found a job, don't let your networking contacts die. They can be valuable business contacts down the road.

MAKE CLASSIFIED ADS A REGULAR PART OF YOUR READING DIET

Even if you are happily employed, it is a good idea to make the classified ads a regular part of your reading diet. This will key you into the companies that are hiring and growing (and the ones that are not). Even more important, it will clue you into the skills considered valuable in the current marketplace. Keeping on top of the latest trends and skills will not only make you more valuable to your current employer, it will make your transition to the job market a smooth one, when that day eventually arrives.

KEEP A SUCCESS FILE

It's an especially good idea to keep an ongoing file of your successes (no matter how seemingly insignificant) and praise you've received. If a co-worker or colleague gives you praise, ask him or her to put it in writing. Be sure to keep a copy of all performance reviews that you receive during your career. This makes a great portfolio for you to base a resume on and is an excellent tool to present in the later stages of job interviewing.

> "It is never too late to be what you might have been."
> —George Eliot, nineteenth century British author

KEEP LEARNING AND GROWING

If possible, it is always a good idea to seek out new responsibilities that are valuable in the job market. Continually test your abilities and take occasional risks. Volunteer for an upcoming project or take on responsibilities that are outside of your current job description. You may even try adopting the dress and demeanor of those you want to impress. I remember the story of a savvy law office clerk who confused her colleagues by dressing more like the lawyers than the office staff. She was the first to volunteer when a lawyer needed a job done quickly and set out to learn as much as she could about her company and her profession. Her strategy eventually earned her a promotion.

It's also a good idea to become a key player in your professional trade association. Volunteer to help out with an upcoming event or run for an elected position. Also, write an article for your trade publication or start a publication or newsletter of your own. Read the latest business books and attend seminars about general career topics (such as, "Assertiveness Training and You") or topics specific to your industry or job. If you don't have the time or budget to attend a seminar, you may choose to listen to seminars on audiotape. Career-Track Seminars has an excellent series of seminars available on audio, some targeted specifically to women. (For more information, write: CareerTrack Seminars, 1800 38th Street, Boulder, CO 80301 or call (303) 447-2300.) In short, keep learning and growing and your career will reap the rewards!

A Final Word

> "If you think you can, you can. And if you think you can't, you're right."
>
> —Mary Kay Ashe

By the time you read this, you should be well into your job search. Hopefully, you're turning up more contacts and job leads every day—and, if not, you're reevaluating and revising your plan. Perhaps you're even interviewing and receiving job offers!

But whatever stage you happen to be at in your job search, realize that you're going to experience some setbacks. You may feel anxious and frustrated, and some days you simply won't want to send out any resumes or make any networking calls. This is normal! But the key, at these times, is to make sure you don't let your job search come to a standstill. If you feel that you need a break, don't stop searching altogether—just slow down the pace for a day or two. Even if you're sending out only one letter or making one phone call, at least you're still making progress.

Job searching is tough for everyone, but if you work hard and focus on your goals, the possibilities are endless! The right job can be a source of great personal satisfaction and is well worth the effort it takes to find it.

Keep trying and keep learning. The rest will fall into place.

Bibliography

— "Economic Penalties of Having Children." *USA Today* (April 1993): 5.

— "Fighting Age-Old Problems." *National Business Employment Weekly* (June 25-July 1, 1993): 24.

— "How Long Will It Take to Find a New Job?" *National Business Employment Weekly* (July 30-August 5, 1993): 15.

— "How to Beat the Job Market." *Fortune* (June 15, 1992): 12.

— "Midsize Firms: The New Job Engine?" *Fortune* (June 14, 1993): 10.

AARP. *Returning to the Job Market: A Woman's Guide to Employment Planning*. Washington, DC: American Association of Retired Persons, 1992.

Adams, Bob and Laura Morin. *The Complete Resume & Job Search Book for College Students*. Holbrook, MA: Bob Adams, Inc., 1992.

Anzelowitz, Lois. "The 25 Hottest Careers." *Working Woman* (July 1993): 41-51.

Asher, Donald. "Ten Telephone Tips." *National Business Employment Weely* (August 6-12, 1993): 5-6.

Baber, Anne and Lynne Waymon. "No-Nonsense Networking." *Your Company* (Summer 1993): 34-38.

Ball, William Andru. *Surviving Unemployment*. Antioch, CA: Ball Research Institute, 1992.

Beamish, Gerry. "Managing Stress During a Job Search." *National Business Employment Weekly* (June 18-24, 1993): 9-10.

Besson, Taunee. "Ten Mistakes to Avoid During Job Interviews." *National Business Employment Weekly* (March 20-26, 1994): 7-8.

Beyer, Cathy, Loretta McGovern, and Doris Pike. *Surviving Unemployment: A Family Handbook for Weathering Hard Times*. New York: Henry Holt, 1993.

Bullock, Edward W. "A Networking Guide for Minority Professionals." *National Business Employment Weekly* (July 30-August 5, 1993): 19-21.

Charland, William, Ph.D. *Career Shifting: Starting Over in a Changing Economy*. Holbrook, MA: Bob Adams, Inc., 1993.

Clymer, Anne W. and Elizabeth McGregor. "Solving the Job Puzzle." *Occupational Outlook Quarterly* (Fall, 1992): 3-6.

Curatola, Anthony P., Ph.D. "Job-Seeking Expenses." *Management Accounting* (June 1992): 9.

Eigles, Lorrie. "How to Find a Job When Your Spouse Relocates." *Women in Business* (January/February 1993): 16.

Fisher, Anne B. "When Will Women Get to the Top?" *Fortune* (September 21, 1992): 44-56.

Fries, James and Ronald Dow. "New CD-ROM Technologies Help the Unemployed Search for Jobs." *American Libraries* (November, 1992): 845.

Jupina, Andrea. "How to Get Search Help Without Breaking the Bank." *National Business Employment Weekly* (July 23-29, 1993): 9-11.

Kirsch, Sandra. "The Job Drought." *Fortune* (August 24, 1992): 62-74.

Logue, Charles H., Ph.D. *Outplace Yourself: Secrets of an Executive Outplacement Counselor*. Holbrook, MA: Bob Adams, Inc., 1993.

Lopez, Julie Amparano. "How Much Did You Earn?" *National Business Employment Weekly* (July 30-August 5, 1993): 29-30.

Mahar, Maggie. "The Truth About Women's Pay." *Working Woman* (April 1993): 52-55, 100-102.

Manniz, Margaret, Susan Lindauer, and Terri Thompson. "Job Scams on the Rise." *U.S. News & World Report* (February 4, 1991): 71.

Miller, Stacey Slaughter. "Get Organized Now!" *National Business Employment Weekly* (July 16-22, 1993): 15-16.

Miller, Stacey Slaughter. "Common Mistakes that Plague Job Hunters." *National Business Employment Weekly* (July 23-29, 1993): 5-6.

Nadler, Burton J. "The Secrets of Job Search Success." *Careers and the College Grad* (1993): 42-43.

Nathanson, Linda Sue. "You Need a Resume Summary." *National Business Employment Weekly* (August 6-12, 1993): 9-10.

O, Dorothy. "How to Job Hunt While You're Still Employed." *National Business Employment Weekly* (July 2-8, 1993): 9-10.

Ricahrdson, Douglas B. "Confessions of a Resume Reader." *National Business Employment Weekly* (June 18-24, 1993): 4-6.

Rist, Neal. "Become a Better Networker." *National Business Employment Weekly* (July 2-8, 1993): 15-16.

Scheele, Adele, Ph.D. "Are You Stressed to the Limit?" *Working Woman* (April 1993): 34, 37.

Scheele, Adele, Ph.D. "Five Simple Ways to Temper the Tension." *Working Woman* (April 1993): 34.

Scheele, Adele, Ph.D. "Job-Hunting Advice for Executives." *Working Woman* (June, 1993): 26.

Smith, Carter, ed. *The National JobBank 1994*. Holbrook, MA: Bob Adams, Inc., 1994.

Stankus, Tony. "The Alert Collector." *RQ* (Winter 1991): 155-160.

Tokay, Mark. "Keeping Your Skills Current." *National Business Employment Weekly* (July 30-August 5, 1993): 9-10.

Yate, Martin. *Knock 'em Dead: The Ultimate Job Seeker's Handbook*. Holbrook, MA: Bob Adams, Inc., 1994.

Zitron, Susan and Sarah McClurg. "Selling Your Skills with a 'Sound Bite.'" *National Business Employment Weekly* (July 9-15, 1993): 5-6.

Index

Job Service, 157-158 *See* also Public employment service

About the Author

Laura Morin graduated from the University of Vermont with a Bachelor's degree in Sociology and Women's Studies. She is a writer and editor, currently working and residing in the Boston area. She is the co-author of *The Complete Resume & Job Search Book for College Students.*

AVAILABLE AT YOUR LOCAL BOOKSTORE

The Adams Jobs Almanac. 920 pages, $15.00

Updated annually, *The Adams Jobs Almanac* provides an unprecedented amount of information on nationwide career opportunities and strategies. This best-selling book includes: names and addresses for over ten thousand leading employers; information on which jobs each company hires for; industry forecasts and geographical cross-references; a close look at over forty popular professions; a detailed forecast of 21st-century careers; and advice on preparing resumes and shining at interviews. It's the most comprehensive national career reference guide available!

The Adams Resume Almanac. 780 pp., $10.95

The Adams Resume Almanac is the most thoroughly researched, most comprehensive resume guide in print. It features detailed information on resume development and layout, a review of the pros and cons of the various formats, an exhaustive review of the strategies that will definitely get a resume noticed, and over 600 sample resumes in dozens of career categories.

The Complete Resume & Job Search Book for College Students. Bob Adams with Laura Morin. 200 pp., $9.95

This guide is the most comprehensive job hunting manual for college students available. From changing indefinite goals into realistic career plans to negotiating salary and benefits, Bob Adams and Laura Morin guide the college student through every step of the career-searching process. Equally important, the book includes plenty of sample resumes and cover letters covering most college majors and many different types of jobs.

The JobBank Series

There are now 20 *JobBank* books, each providing extensive, up-to-date employment information on hundreds of the largest employers in each job market. Recommended as an excellent place to begin your job search by *The New York Times, The Los Angeles Times, The Boston Globe, The Chicago Tribune,* and many other publications, JobBank books have been used by hundreds of thousands of people to find jobs.

Books available: *The Atlanta JobBank—The Boston JobBank—The Carolina JobBank—The Chicago JobBank—The Dallas/Fort Worth JobBank—The Denver JobBank—The Detroit JobBank—The Florida JobBank—The Houston JobBank—The Los Angeles JobBank—The Minneapolis/St. Paul JobBank—The New York JobBank—The Ohio JobBank—The Philadelphia JobBank—The Phoenix JobBank—The St. Louis JobBank—The San Francisco JobBank—The Seattle JobBank—The Tennessee JobBank—The Washington D.C. JobBank.* Each book is over 300 pages, paperback, and $15.95.

If you cannot find a book at your local bookstore, you may order it directly from the publisher. Please send payment including $4.50 for shipping and handling (for the entire order) to: Bob Adams, Inc., 260 Center Street, Holbrook, MA 02343. Credit card holders may call 1-800-USA-JOBS (in Massachusetts, 617-767-8100).